Who wants a dog!

Who wants a dog !

P. J. Whyte

DAVID & CHARLES
Newton Abbot   London

First published in the Republic of South Africa by
Juta and Company Limited, Cape Town

This edition first published in the United Kingdom in 1980 by
David & Charles (Publishers) Ltd, Newton Abbot, Devon

Illustrated by

British Library Cataloguing in Publication Data

Whyte, P J
  Who wants a dog! - 2nd ed.
  1. Dogs
  I. Title
  636.7'08'3   SF427

  ISBN 0-7153-7939-9

Printed in Great Britain
by Redwood Burn Limited, Trowbridge & Esher
for David & Charles (Publishers) Limited
Brunel House Newton Abbot Devon

CONTENTS

ACKNOWLEDGEMENTS

My sincere thanks go to Dr Ian du Toit
and Serita Swanepoel.

'Mutty'

FOREWORD

Every veterinarian dealing daily with numbers of dogs will bear witness to the number of unhappy and maladjusted dogs and their owners. There are a number of reasons for this, starting with the selection of the wrong kind of dog for their purposes and thus having wrong expectations from their pet, and in not understanding their dog fully they become disillusioned with it and give it less and less attention. This causes the dog to be more and more difficult and unhappy.

The author, who specializes in the corrective training of problem dogs, is already well known. This book deals with every aspect of owning a dog, from the selection of the correct type of dog for your purpose to understanding health and breeding problems and from the basic necessities of training to more advanced training. It fills a great gap in the literature about dogs and should find itself a place in every home where dogs are kept. There is something in it for everyone, from those who have never owned a dog before to those who are well acquainted with them.

The author has gone to great lengths to ensure that all the facts in this book are correct, and it is hoped that it will enable us to look forward to better balanced and adjusted patients and happier owners.

CHAPTER 1

CHOOSING THE RIGHT DOG

So, you're looking for a dog? You'll be wanting him to be with you for a good ten to fifteen years, and to bring you much pleasure. But there's such an assortment of shapes and sizes amongst dogs, and it's headaches, not happiness, a dog brings when the wrong one is chosen! And how easy it is to choose the wrong dog when an adorable, fluffy little bundle waddles up to you and licks your toes. And how quickly that adorable, fluffy little bundle can turn into a boisterous, stubborn and noisy animal that brings more problems than pleasure!

Many of these dogs—which a family was once so happy to acquire—are taken to vets and animal sanctuaries to be put down or given away. So—for the sake of yourself, and your children who will grow to love your dog, and, most of all, for the sake of the dog himself who may not get another chance—choose your dog carefully.

Then there are the inconveniences of owning a dog: getting up earlier than usual on a Sunday to take him out, having to clean up mud and hair after him when the weather's unfavourable and grooming's neglected, puddles for the first few weeks, wild greetings when you come home, and . . . a glance at chapter 17 on problem dogs will give you a glimpse of what else you may be letting yourself in for!

A dog consumes time and money, and he's lively and demanding—to put it shortly, he's a nuisance! I won't go into all the *advantages* of owning a dog, because if you hadn't already known them you wouldn't have bought this book!

However, should you still remain undaunted, here's a guide to help you choose the right dog for yourself.

(a) A Dog to Suit your Circumstances

1. *A dog consumes time*

Most breeds—except perhaps toy breeds—need daily exercise. Terriers and large dogs in need of a good run may let loose excess energy on you and your property by chewing, digging, sending you and your children flying with over-exuberant eagerness, or by constant yapping. Some of the long-haired breeds also take up time. Without care, their coats become knotted and dull, they smell or shed loose hair in the home.

2. *A dog costs money to keep*

The cost of a dog may be negligible compared with his upkeep over the years. The bigger the dog, the more his food will cost you. Vet's bills can mount up alarmingly; holiday-time means kennelling costs; and breeds such as *Poodles*, *Terriers*, and so on, need to be clipped or trimmed from time to time—and unless you do it yourself that's not for nothing, either.

3. *A dog needs space*

Have you room for the breed of your choice? It's not only the size of the dog you should consider, but the purpose for which he was bred. A *King Charles Spaniel*, for instance, bred to be pampered, will settle down better in a flat than some smaller dogs, such as *Scotties*, which were bred for sport. A *Great Dane* is better suited to a suburban home than a *Doberman* which was bred for police work. Hounds (*Dachshunds*, *Beagles* and *Bassets*, for example) and Terriers are hunters. Toy breeds are lap-dogs. *Alsatians* are working dogs, *Bull Terriers* are fighters. *Border Collies* are herders (of sheep, children, other dogs, cars and bicycles alike). And who knows better than the *Peke* himself that he was bred over thousands of years to be admired and indulged?

Some breeds, however, have been modified over the years—notably *Bulldogs*, long-haired *Collies*, *Great Danes* and *Setters*, which are now bred more for their beauty than for their working ability. A dog that's been bred for a long time for his looks alone is less likely to need an outlet for his working or hunting instincts, and should therefore be better able to settle down to a more confined way of life. If, for example, you don't bring

home a bull for your *Bulldog* to bait from time to time—
he'll forgive you!

When we choose the wrong breed for our purpose, *he*
is penalized for doing what he was originally intended
to do—and nobody wants him. The very feature which
brought him and us together originally (his working,
herding, guarding or hunting instinct) is now so often his
downfall, and *he*, of course, gets the blame! This is why
so many *Bull Terriers* fight, *Bassets* roam, *Terriers* yap,
Collies chase cars and *Alsatians* bite passers-by.

4. *A dog needs companionship and affection*

A dog is, by his very nature, sociable. He has both an
alert and capable brain and an affectionate nature. Long
hours spent alone are very bleak for him—and a waste
of potential, considering just what dogs are capable of.
The companionship he asks is nothing compared to
what he has to give.

No dog should be left alone for long stretches—a pup
not only needs his midday meal but he's been used to
company twenty-four hours a day. An adult dog becomes
miserable, destructive, or unmanageable when he's left
alone a lot. Those who go out often will find a toy breed
easy to take with them—in fact he'll enjoy the outings.
And for those who are out all day, a pair of cats are
more suitable companions.

(b) A Dog to Suit your Purpose

1. *A watch-dog*

How many people become disillusioned with their
dog because he slept while the house was burgled?

Dogs, like people, have different abilities. Some dogs
are gifted with the ability to protect, others to retrieve,
to be easily trained, to follow a trail—and so on. These
abilities can, of course, be deliberately bred into a dog,

14

A watchdog

but it's a skilled and time-consuming process. We shall have to be content with choosing a watch-dog from the sources available to us.

The usual procedure when getting a watch-dog is to buy a large dog and take it for granted he'll be on twenty-four hours a day guard duty. But the dog, if he's to be completely suitable, should be properly selected — unless of course, you just happen to be lucky!

Various families have different ideas about what they expect from a watch-dog. Some want an alert dog that gives the alarm; others want a dog that looks fierce, but would never bite; and then there are those that want a dog with a well-developed guarding instinct.

In giving the alarm, most Terriers, toys and other small dogs excel themselves. As smaller dogs usually have better hearing than bigger dogs, their sharp and persistent yapping can generally be depended on to give intruders second thoughts. But, as they're inclined to be indiscriminate in giving their warnings, this can have its disadvantages!

Getting a dog that looks fierce, but would never bite, presents no difficulties. For example, *Dalmatians* are large but don't usually bite; the slight type of *Boxer* has a reputation for being most benign to mankind in general, but can always be depended on to look most forbidding; *Bulldogs* are known for their exceptionally good nature, but look terrifying. Another good-natured dog that also looks terrifying is a *Chow*—he is a rather lovable, serious dog. *Great Danes* have not been bred to attack, and if they do become actively protective, they usually corner and hold their victim, without actually biting (so I'm told, but don't ask me to prove it!). Their appearance alone will put fear into the bravest heart. Great Danes are extremely good-natured dogs.

Lastly, getting a dog with a well-developed guarding instinct presents many difficulties. You can buy a fully-trained guard dog; or choose an adult dog that shows potential; or do as most people do, and take a chance with a pup.

In the first place, the average family is not advised to buy a dog that's been trained to attack. An attack-trained dog can be dangerous, unless he's been very skilfully and wisely trained—and unless you, personally, can handle such a dog.

In the second place, buying a pup in the hopes that he'll grow into a good watch-dog may be a bit of a gamble. The best you can do is to choose from one of the breeds discussed below, viewing litters of dogs that show the desired characteristics. Unfortunately, it cannot be guaranteed that their offspring have actually inherited these desirable qualities.

We can conclude then, that when you buy a pup—you

may indeed be 'sold a pup'! The best guide (but only a guide, and not a guarantee) is firstly, to see the pup's parents, and secondly, to see any previous litters they may have had to see if they *are* passing on their good qualities. But these may be scattered far and wide, and not possible to trace.

And lastly, buying a fully-grown dog that shows potential: this is the best proposition when obtaining a watch-dog, because you can *see* what he's like.

When you are buying a pup, try to avoid one that has been too inbred. This is discussed in the chapter on breeding.

You obtain a fully grown dog by

(1) contacting the rescue societies which are run by many breed clubs to place dogs whose owners can for some reason no longer keep them;
(2) watching the pets' column in the small ads section of your local paper;
(3) visiting the various animal sanctuaries in your district;
(4) visiting breeding kennels.

The first three suggestions are the best, since breeding kennels don't usually keep a selection of fully-grown dogs because of the expense involved.

When you're choosing a suitable watch-dog, avoid one that is nervous or, on the other hand, *too* friendly, giving all and sundry a wild greeting! And (if you're viewing him at an animal sanctuary) a dog that holds his head down, seeking an escape route, is usually a calculating dog and more likely to put his own interests first.

If you see a dog that stands firmly upright, looking you directly in the eye, he's probably a sensible, intelligent dog. If you're viewing him at a private home, he should regard you with suspicion, placing himself between you and his present owner. Take your time finding him—he'll be with you for another ten to twelve years.

Be sure that the dog you're considering isn't being got rid of because he's vicious. And if he's good with children, so much the better—a good family guard is nearly always good with children.

(The section on choosing a dog for training gives further guidance on how to judge a dog's temperament.)

Good watch-dogs are to be found amongst several different breeds, and below are some of the merits and otherwise of a few.

Because *German Shepherds* (*Alsatians*) were originally bred to protect sheep, a good specimen is an excellent watch-dog. Even though this breed is the victim of a lot of adverse publicity, they have for a long time topped the sales charts in most Western countries.

They are used extensively as guide dogs for the blind, as rescue dogs (no other breed is used in the Austrian Alps), and, of course, as police and war dogs. They could not have such a record were they not an outstanding breed. The reasons why they have such a bad name are probably, firstly, because they outnumber other breeds; secondly, they are news-value; thirdly, they are not always properly controlled and do bite while protecting their families; and, lastly, there are unfortunately those that have been unwisely bred.

Correctly bred, raised and handled, a German Shepherd need never be taught to guard his family— only not to be so earnest about it! He's ever watchful and alert, particularly where children are concerned. But it is *because* he's such an outstanding dog that he gives his owners so much more—whether it's more pleasure, or more trouble, depends on how he's handled and cared for.

How can you avoid buying an inferior German

Shepherd? Firstly, the dog (or his parents if you're buying a pup) shouldn't show any unreasonable fear if you're hoping to use him as a watch-dog. A German Shepherd is a naturally cautious dog, but he should not turn and run at the approach of a stranger. Secondly, he should be both loving and submissive towards his family—and, thirdly, a fully-grown German Shepherd should be somewhat wary of strangers.

Those that are long of limb and slightly built are not usually as protective as the stockier Alsatian. The very heavy dog, however, may also be less protective, but his size compensates for this! The very large, lumbering type of German Shepherd is usually an extremely gentle dog—although he is, for some reason, condemned in show circles. He makes a fine pet. Those of average build with shorter legs and fluid movements are natural family guards. And, lastly, the very fluffy Alsatian is usually rather independent and often less protective.

I've noticed when training German Shepherds that their colouring as well as their build may be a guide when judging their temperament. The plain white or plain black dogs, although nearly always protective, are

... as police dogs ...

19

usually more strong-willed than the black and tan or tan and brown Alsatians. I've also found that the lighter tan-coloured dogs are usually very protective toward their families. Temperament also appears to be linked with eye colour. Those with deeper coloured eyes seem to be more adaptable, and those with light coloured eyes are usually more intense and strong-willed than those with darker eyes.

Boxers and *Dobermans* are of either a light or a heavy build. The heavy types of each of these breeds usually make very good watch-dogs. However, they're not suitable for many people. The large Doberman is an extremely powerful animal and should be kept only on a small-holding or a farm, unless his owner has the time to give him very adequate exercise. He is a magnificent dog if properly kept and correctly trained, but a potential menace when too confined. The light (in weight, not colour) type of Doberman is, however, quite different. He is usually a nervous dog. This reduced bone structure is probably the result of too much inbreeding.

The large Boxer, also powerfully built, has a very strong character and can become fiercely protective, needing both adequate exercise (a problem, because he's so often a fighter) and very firm handling. The more narrow-chested type of Boxer, however, is light-hearted and full of fun.

Border Collies usually make excellent watch-dogs, but their protective spirit can get out of hand if they're not properly controlled. They're a very strong-willed breed — deceptively so because of their gentleness. (The section on choosing a dog to train discusses Border Collies in more detail.)

Labradors can also be extremely good watch-dogs — an aspect of this excellent breed that is often underestimated. The various types of Labrador are also discussed in the section on choosing a dog to train — the watch-dog type is a perfect family guard.

A *Bull Terrier* is, broadly speaking, a dog for the Bull Terrier enthusiast. Although he's an excellent watch-dog, he can become very fierce. Bull Terriers are an extremely strong-willed breed of dog. Those who know them, however, will have no other! Animal lovers fall under the categories of: cat lovers, dog lovers—or Bull Terrier lovers! As one Bull Terrier owner was once told—'Man—there's a lot of *dog* in that dog!'

. . . a lot of dog . . .

Temperaments amongst Bull Terriers may vary slightly. The short, stocky, white Bull Terrier is usually more stubborn than the brown, more long-legged type of dog.

Keeshonds can also be fierce, but these dogs, too, I recommend only to those who know the breed. I have a number brought to me by owners who are unused to them and find them difficult to handle. Once again, however, those who know the breed find no other like them.

Bouviers. Here is another very good watch-dog. But Bouviers need space, exercise and firmness. Although they are bold dogs, they're also sensitive and loving—but often strong-willed.

Weimeraners are fast becoming popular, and they're gaining a reputation for protecting their families very well.

Ridgebacks are a fine breed of dog, when properly bred and properly handled. The large, heavy type of Ridgeback needs very firm handling, because he can become very fierce. The lighter type of Ridgeback is usually an affectionate, friendly dog.

Cross-breeds and *mongrels* can be intensely loyal and extremely protective towards their families. They are often quite outstanding watch-dogs.

When you've acquired your watch-dog, turn to page 56, where you'll find advice on how best to help your fully-grown dog settle down in his new home.

A dog that's actively protective should not be allowed to play with a crowd of children. When the children chase and rough-and-tumble one another, he may be prompted to take his duties too seriously, and a child may get bitten.

The best way for a dog to develop a feeling of protectiveness towards his home and family is for him to be given the run of the house. Also, if he sleeps indoors he's not easily disposed of by anyone who doesn't wish you well—and he has an added advantage over an intruder when let loose.

Should you be disappointed with your dog because he appears afraid, remember that no dog can be altogether without fear. A certain amount is a natural reaction in every animal, and is necessary for the survival of the species.

Some dogs show less fear than others. German Shepherds, for instance, are usually more cautious than Dobermans—but this makes them easier to train, because they don't have such a resistance to correction. (A good German Shepherd, however, shows virtually no fear when his master is threatened—but when he himself is threatened, he is more submissive.) When a

German Shepherd is trained by a skilled trainer, his courage can be developed to its full potential.

I'm often asked: 'If I discipline my puppy, will it break his spirit so that he won't guard me when he's fully grown?' 'If I tell my dog to stop barking, will it make him not bark when an intruder comes?' 'If he's friendly with visitors will it make him too friendly with intruders?' 'If I show him too much love, will he become useless as a guard?' The answer to all four questions is—'No'.

How can you teach a dog to be ever ready to come between his owner and danger? You can't. Either he has the potential to be protective, or he hasn't—whether he's pedigreed, cross-bred or mongrel, big or small. We won't go into the process of actually teaching a dog to attack because of the obvious dangers involved. For instance, a dog that's been taught to attack may be triggered off by a signal—such as running or screaming, a waving stick, or the sight of a gun. Children can easily inadvertently trigger a dog into attacking if he hasn't been properly trained—or if he hasn't the ability to distinguish real danger from play.

A novice may try to make his dog protective by keeping him out of doors (he often does the reverse then, and becomes independent); or by chaining him up (he is then useful only in a limited area, and may even lose his spirit altogether—or, on the other hand, release his pent-up energy by biting *anyone* when let loose); or by teasing him (a dog that's teased can become extremely dangerous and attack or bite indiscriminately); or by keeping him hungry (he'll probably be so preoccupied with looking for food that he'll not be much use as a guard).

If you want your dog to protect you, firstly, choose a

dog that is a natural family protector; secondly, allow him to regard himself as one of the family and, thirdly, praise him when he begins to bark and show signs of protectiveness towards you. And if he gets *too* protective —train him!

2. *A dog as a companion*

If you are choosing a dog as a companion for yourself, I must point out that those who come to me with problems resulting from owning a dog that is unsuitable for them are mostly people from the older section of the public or those with small children. The former usually own large dogs, either because they're fashionable, or because they afford protection, or because they are a breed they are accustomed to owning over the years. But one needs strength to cope with the boisterousness of large dogs—even if they *are* well-behaved. Unsatisfactory relationships and forced partings causing heartbreak on the part of both dog and owner are the result of many of these mismatchings. (The compatibility of a dog and his owner is discussed in detail later in the chapter.)

For those who are newly-married a pup is a wonderful companion, but, so often, along comes the time when there's a fourth member of the family, and the dog proves to be quite unsuitable. Large dogs, generally so fond of children, are not aware of their own weight. Even *Bull Terriers* and *Bassets*, which are not so big, are very heavy and can get far too rough with crawling babies and toddlers.

On the other hand, the breed chosen by the newly-weds may be a fragile toy breed, and although he proved to be ideal for them when they bought him, the new addition thinks he's one of his stuffed teddy bears and the mother wishes she'd bought a more sturdy breed of dog—and so does the dog!

In practice, it is much better not to get a dog when you have, or are expecting, a new baby.

When Pup grows up and suddenly finds he's not the only youngster in the family any more, this is when, so often, he waits for his walk in vain, dinner is late and he's pushed out of doors most of the time. He becomes a nuisance through no fault of his own, whereas he used to be very much loved 'one and only'.

If his place of priority in the heart of his owners becomes usurped, he should still be fitted into the family scene. Most of all, he should be disciplined so that he doesn't lie on Junior and lick him as soon as he's accessible to the adoring dog, but obeys commands to restrain his display of affection. A few reprimands are easily understood and far kinder than banishment to where Baby becomes someone to look at longingly from outside.

If your children are still small (or if there's likely to be a small addition before Pup is mature) and you want a big dog, remember that the tiny little bundle of *Alsatian*, *Labrador*, *Great Dane* or *Boxer* will soon be triple your child's weight. Even when Pup is still *half* your child's size, Baby usually comes off second best in a playful romp! Many a dog has lost a loving home that way.

Some people consider *Bull Terriers* among the most gentle breeds with children and would never recommend a greyhound but I have found that of the larger breeds, *Greyhounds*, *Dalmatians*, *Border Collies* and *Rough Collies* are the most gentle. Unlike so many of the larger breeds, they seem to be aware of their own weight when they're playing with children. Greyhounds are perfect children's pets—they're extremely gentle and adore children, often singling them out in a crowd. They should not, however, be placed with a boisterous family.

Dalmatians are dogs with an exceptional capacity for expressing devotion without being soppy. Border Collies instinctively love and protect children. (The problems that may arise from owning a Border Collie are discussed in the section on choosing a dog to train.) Lastly, Rough Collies, like Greyhounds, should not be placed with boisterous children. They're sensitive and gentle and are also very playful and affectionate.

When you're selecting a dog as a pet for your children, the age of the children, and the space available, are the main deciding factors when choosing a breed.

A young boy with access to open country, who wants a dog to go horse-riding with him will enjoy, among the larger breeds, a *Labrador*, *Dalmatian*, *German Shepherd*, *Border Collie*, *Boxer* or *mongrel*, to mention a few. The fact that the dog will get ample exercise means that almost any breed will settle down well and bring much happiness. (If you choose a German Shepherd or a Labrador, try to ensure that he is free of hip dysplasia, or he won't stand up to the exercise. See page 123).

Among the smaller breeds, a sturdy *Schipperke* (not one bred from nervous and undersized parents), *Irish Terriers*, *Fox Terriers* (the rough-haired variety show a stronger will than the smooth-haired) are all very companionable and sporty. Once again, it's a matter for personal preference.

A girl may like a more cuddly dog rather than a sporty one. The toy breeds, of course, spring to mind. But not all toys are suitable—they're often highly strung and intolerant of the demands of children.

A *Poodle* can be a wonderful little companion. His awareness and appealing ways make him a joy to own. Be careful, however, not to buy one from hysterical and over-excited parents.

Don't buy any dog if he'll have to be left alone a lot—especially a Poodle—he's a dog that needs ample companionship and attention; and if you haven't the time and money to brush him every few days, and clip him every five to seven weeks—also think twice. A Poodle has a lot to give, but he also needs a lot of time, attention and affection.

A *Dachshund* is another dog which, provided he's handled gently, makes a lovely children's pet. He's a charming little dog, often strong-willed and always brimming with personality. (No overfeeding please!)

Toy Poms and *Maltese* are also very playful and appealing—they're delightful little dogs and make very attractive additions to any home. But if there are children in the house, they should be placed with them only if they are going to be gentle with the dog—they are dogs that know how to stick up for themselves!

Chihuahuas are the smallest dogs in the world and, like Poodles, should be given lots of love and attention.

It's a big world when you're so small, and you need to be looked after! Chihuahuas are courageous little dogs, considering their size. They're intelligent, lively and playful.

Sealyhams, *Scotties* and *Cairn Terriers* are three breeds from the Isles that have won the hearts of many. All three are characters that don't easily take 'no' for an answer, and should be well disciplined from puppy-hood. They also need plenty of exercise. The Cairn is not as well known as the Sealyham and Scottie, but is probably the least strong-willed of the three, and his scruffy face and cheeky eyes make him an irresistible pet.

Spaniels are very beautiful and adoring dogs, but can also be very excitable and strong-willed. When buying a Spaniel, choose carefully from parents that are not excitable or too inbred, and that are good with children.

... the smallest breed ...

Corgis are dogs with tremendous appeal. They are beautiful and have charming ways. But once they're in, they rule the house! A Corgi has a mind of his own, and once it's made up it won't be easily changed! They are sweet and loving dogs—but usually strong-willed.

A *Schipperke* is an ideal pet. If gently handled, he's the essence of gentleness with children and is also an excellent little watch-dog. His coat doesn't need much care, he doesn't get boisterous if he misses his walk and except perhaps for his tendency to yap, he is an excellent companion.

However, a Schipperke that has been bred from highly

strung and under-sized parents is altogether a different dog. A miniature Schipperke, although very loving and appealing, is generally an excitable dog, and not as easy to handle.

English and *Staffordshire Bull Terriers*, *Boxers*, *Great Danes* and *German Shepherds* are all very good with children, but are usually very rough while maturing. From the age of about four to eighteen months, these large breeds, unless they are properly disciplined, are usually quite incompatible with toddlers.

A *German Shepherd* (Alsatian) is a wonderful dog for children. Properly bred and handled, he is a superior dog—and for this very reason should be raised and trained with care. There are not many dogs to match a German Shepherd's preoccupation with the safety of his small charges. On beaches and in parks they can always be seen on outings with their families, constantly running back to check that all is well with the children, then off to play, and back to check again. I've seen no other breed of dog do this so consistently.

A *Labrador's* love of children is taken for granted. He simply glows with goodwill towards all children—but he's also inclined to underestimate his own strength. A Labrador is a dog with an outstanding personality. He has a lovely nature, and sensible (in most cases!) disposition, lots of character, and most appealing facial expressions.

Irish Setters are affectionate and gentle. They are very fond of children, but need regular brushing and plenty of exercise.

If, once you've acquired your dog, play is tactfully supervised, your child will learn that Pup is not a new toy, and Pup that Baby is not a litter mate with tough hide to withstand needle-like teeth and boisterous tumbling. Not only will the child not get hurt, but your dog will grow up to adore children, and they'll derive much pleasure from each other.

If their play is not disciplined, however, and they're left to sort out their differences themselves, your dog may grow up to mistrust all children if he's roughly handled. If Pup plays too roughly — or worse, nips in self-defence — a child may get badly hurt and the dog pay heavily for it, possibly with his life. Children can be very cruel, and pups very rough. If both the child is disciplined not to hurt the dog, and the dog not to be too rough, both will, in the long run, benefit. However, other children may not be as gentle with dogs as you've taught yours to be. A few moments' experience with rough children may leave an impression that will last him the rest of his life.

Before a mother takes the decision to acquire a new pup, she should first consider whether she can fit a pup's many needs into her already busy routine and tolerate the inconveniences that accompany his arrival — attend to his three meals a day, see that he has peace when he needs to sleep, put up with messes in the house, chewed possessions, missing toys and lots of other puppy mischief besides — because that's what the addition of this new little family member will entail.

Where the presence or possibility of young children or senior citizens need not be considered, the selection of a suitable breed is much wider. Other sections in this chapter discuss the merits and otherwise of several other breeds in detail. However, it is only fair to add that these are very subjective assessments based on dogs I've known. Different strains may show different characteristics and you should always try to make an assessment of the individual dog's potential from the character of the parents and other adults the breeder has produced.

3. *A dog to show*

It's not very often that a pup displaying the qualities of a potential beauty champion is sold as a pet. You either pay a huge sum for a possible or proven champ or set up a kennel with expensive foundation stock and breed him yourself—probably after several years and, even then, only if you're lucky.

If, however, you remain undaunted and would like to launch yourself into the fiercely competitive world of dog shows, take the time and trouble to attend shows and read books on the breed of your choice before you buy your dog.

And if he never wins a show, you'll know that it's not *his* fault that the chap who wrote down the conformations required in a champion didn't happen to include the physical attributes of your particular pet. You'll love him just the same! (Show dogs are discussed in more detail on page 268. If you're wanting to show your dog, he should be registered by his breeder *before* he is three months old.

4. *A dog to train*

If you're buying a dog with a view to joining a training club and pursuing this enjoyable sport, it's not important what your dog *looks* like. What *is* important, though, is that he has a loving and submissive temperament, and an alert manner. Submissiveness isn't essential, however, but an amateur will find a tractable dog much easier to train.

When you set out to acquire your dog, follow the procedure suggested for seeking a watch-dog, but instead of seeking a bold dog you should look for one that's friendly. However, be careful not to get a dog that's too excitable—highly excitable dogs are very difficult for an amateur to train.

What about intelligence? Well, all dogs are intelligent, whatever their owners may say to the contrary! A dog with average intelligence, however, is more easily trained than one with a high I.Q., because those of

... a little too smart for most people ...

extra brain-power are usually smart enough to put their owners at a disadvantage.

The owner himself, if he's to train his dog successfully, should have quick responses, patience and a calm disposition. And he must, of course, love his dog. Firmness is an asset, as only a very tractable dog can be handled to perfection by a gentle owner. A compatible combination of dog and owner is also important. This is discussed later on in the chapter.

However, should you already have a dog that's suitable for training, rather than burden yourself with all the added trouble of an extra dog, train him. Then when you do get your new dog, you will have already gained some experience.

Although not all dogs can be classified according to personality-type, the following classification of some of the larger breeds can be used as a basic guide as to how different dogs adapt to being trained:

(1) *A bold and steady dog, capable of defending his master*. This dog is reliable and sensible, and usually off-hand with strangers. Provided he's not allowed to become bored, he seldom needs to be trained. If he gets bored, however, he'll seek an outlet for his capabilities, and will then need a firm hand in training. Guide and police dogs are of this type— but when they belong to families that don't exercise and train them properly, the dogs seek an outlet for their intelligence, and their owners usually find they can't handle them and have to get rid of them. *Alsatians* are an excellent example of this type of dog. It's not that the dog isn't good enough for *them—they* are not up to handling their dog!

(2) *A nervous dog, born nervous or become that way through some unfortunate experience*. This type of dog should be handled with a gentle firmness, calmly, and with the utmost patience, receiving ample praise and virtually no physical correction.

(3) *An excitable dog*. The zest for living that an excitable dog has is so often the despair of his owner but, when properly handled, is the delight of his trainer because he so enjoys his lessons. An excitable dog needs clear-cut instructions, modulated praise and sharp corrections—sometimes because he's trying *too* hard! The trainer of an excitable dog must be very firm. He must also be calm and relaxed, because his dog quickly reflects a ruffled attitude.

(4) *A submissive, willing and gentle dog*. A submissive dog, as described above, is the easiest dog for an amateur to train. A well-built *German Shepherd* bitch, long in body and short in limb, usually falls into this category.

(5) *A tough, resilient, stubborn, courageous dog, pleasing himself before he pleases his family.* This type of dog has a 'devil-may-care' outlook on life, and can be trained only by a skilled trainer or a person with a very strong character. If, for instance, he's being viewed at an animal sanctuary, instead of giving the visitors a wild greeting, he'll be looking to see if he can take this chance to get out.

He's a very independent fellow, fearing very little —except perhaps losing his independence. A dog of this type has an extremely high threshold of correction, and unless it is reached he cannot be brought under control. Once this threshold is reached, however, he takes a ligher correction.

So, firstly, he must receive a correction he finds worth avoiding. Secondly, his praise must be very excessive to compete with all the things that interest him. Your third tool is repetition. Lastly, he must have an outlet for his instincts. He must be given a daily walk preferably off the lead—or he won't be easy to train. This, I know, is a vicious circle because he can't be trained until he's adequately exercised,

Good luck to you if you're set on training Mr Lazy Bones!

and he can't be adequately exercised until he's trained. If you have a dog like this, first concentrate on teaching him to come when he's called, and then work from there.

(6) *A very intelligent dog, with a fox-like face.* This dog is usually of slender build and long of limb with slinking movements. He has long pointed ears and close-set, penetrating eyes. He's an exceptionally clever dog—too clever for most people to train! *Alaskan Malmites* and some of the long-legged type of *Alsatian* with sharp pointed ears and long snipy nose fall into this category.

(7) *A large, amiable and lazy dog.* The picture of this type of dog springs readily to mind—and he's the very devil to train, with his slow, ambling movements! He's usually too lazy to be naughty—so it doesn't matter too much anyway.

(8) *A proud, gentle and sensitive dog.* The ancient breeds fall into this category: *Greyhounds, Borzois, Afghans* and *Salukis,* for example. There are also some less venerable breeds that fit into this category, such as *Pointers* and *English Setters.*

These dogs don't usually react to training in the conventional way. They usually give the trainer a cool eye and say they think the whole business is beneath them. Excitable behaviour is usually beneath them, too, so they don't often get out of hand. These dogs should live their lives close to their owner, thereby growing up to be obedient. They don't adapt very easily to formal training—they conform more through love.

(9) *Vicious dogs.* A dog may be vicious only when someone comes too near his owner.

However, if a dog is displaying indiscriminate viciousness, he should be put to sleep. Such a dog is not only an unsuitable pet but may seriously injure, or even kill someone. (The chapter on problem dogs will give you guidance on controlling an over-protective dog.)

Now, let's have an overall look at how some of the more popular breeds react to being trained.

When considering size, you'll find a medium- to large-sized dog easiest to handle. Some small dogs train extremely well, but all the bending involved can be rather hard on the back! Very large dogs, on the other hand, for example *Great Danes*, *Pyrenean Mountain dogs*, *St. Bernards* or *Bloodhounds*, have slower reactions than average-sized dogs, and allowance must be made for this.

German Shepherds (Alsatians), being working dogs, are about the easiest dogs to train. They *want* to be trained, and provided they're not nervous, and are correctly handled, they learn with a single-minded eagerness and astonishing ease.

Border Collies. These dogs are also working dogs. They not only *want* to work, they have a *compulsion* to work. But this compulsion can get out of hand, and if they don't *have* something to do they'll *find* something to do — usually something you don't want done!

Border Collies have lightning-quick responses, and a gentle nature which often belies a very resilient spirit. When you choose a Border Collie, look at his eyes (when buying a pup, look at the eyes of his parents), and choose a dog that has deeper coloured eyes, without too hard a stare. When their eyes are light coloured and piercing, their restless spirit is usually more pronounced.

36

A Border Collie is a dog that must have very adequate exercise; and training is an excellent substitute for his urge to herd. His lessons should be brisk with firm, decisive handling. A well-built Collie is easier to train than an undersized, flimsy one. The flimsy Collies are often nervous and excitable.

A *Standard Poodle* is also very well suited to training, but, if you're not careful, he'll have his own private game with you—so watch out for being outwitted! However, unlike many other clever dogs that can get really naughty, he just has a sense of fun.

A sturdy Standard Poodle is easier to train than a highly bred Poodle with a long snipy nose. If you're firm and patient, a Standard Poodle can be trained with ease. But consider getting a Standard Poodle only if you have the time and money to keep him groomed.

Labradors, from my experience, fit into category numbers (1), (5) or (7) listed above. Those in category (1) are often used as police or guide dogs. Those in category (5) give their owners a headache—but can respond well when trained as suggested. And good luck to you if you're set on training 'Mr Lazy Bones'!

You can't tell what a Labrador will be like while he's still a pup, but if you're choosing an adult dog you can tell by his eyes (or by his corpulence). I have usually found Black Labradors a little more placid and less strong-willed than the Yellow Labradors.

Dobermans, provided they're not of the small, nervous type, are excellent dogs for training. A large Doberman has a superior mentality, and he is powerfully built, but it certainly isn't everyone who can handle him. This is the reason why so many people who buy a Doberman pup find they cannot keep him when he grows up. Their bodies are big, their hearts are big, their needs are big, they need big owners and big grounds. Confine them, and you not only cannot develop their potential, you've got troubles! This is particularly the case with male

Dobermans. The females are not as strong as the males, but they still need space, exercise and discipline.

Mongrels. During my experiences while training dogs; I've found most mongrels easy to train—I haven't had many that have been difficult. But, because of the large variety of dogs found amongst them, I can't commit myself further than that.

Boxers, unless properly disciplined from puppyhood, are not usually easy to train. They either put on a big frown and dig in their heels or work slowly and reluctantly, looking very badly done by—making a dash for it the very first chance they get! However, there are some that, provided they're very attached to their owners and are handled with firmness and patience, can train extremely well—especially if they've been properly disciplined from puppyhood.

Great Danes. A Great Dane is both strong *and* sensitive, and he has slower reactions than dogs of smaller build. Unless you're also strong, you may have difficulty training a dog as big as a Great Dane.

Should he become confused or upset during training you may never regain his confidence again—so handle him with the good old formula of patience and firmness. Keep relaxed and go slowly when training a Great Dane, and be careful never to lose his confidence, always praising his every effort.

Bouviers, like Great Danes, are strong and sensitive, with slower responses. Their temperament is not unlike a Great Dane's, and they can be trained with the same approach.

Ridgebacks are either large and sturdy or light and slender. The larger type of Ridgeback is more stubborn than the lighter type—possibly needing more repetition and praise than most dogs.

Huskies. In order to understand sledge dogs—Huskies and Malamutes, for example—we must remember the tough lives for which they were originally bred.

These dogs were not pampered domestic pets and the sledge dog probably retains much of his wolf-like character. A wolf is an animal not submissive to man—he is submissive to his own kind. This much-maligned animal is highly alert and extremely intelligent; he has initiative, and incredible intuition—which are admirable qualities, but not qualities that make a dog a suitable pet in our civilized situation. If you want a Husky—*you* must adapt to *him*. To train him is to insult him. A Husky's delight is freedom, speed, activity, independence and even hardship and privation, rather than to be subjected into submission to his owner.

An Eskimo doesn't own his dogs—the pack leader owns them. And the Eskimo doesn't command his pack leader—they make decisions together. Hardly a dog for our situation!

A *Chow* is not usually an easy dog to train, although I have encountered the odd exception. He's generally a little indifferent to the endearments of his owners, and therefore doesn't work as eagerly for his rewards as most dogs do. He is, however, a very lovable (and independent) breed of dog. I wouldn't train a Chow for sport, but if he's disobedient and needs to be trained, approach him as suggested for dogs in category (5), and don't train him any more than you need to.

Bull Mastiffs are slow dogs because of their heavy build, and because of their strength and energy need lots of space and exercise. They are also tough *and* sensitive — a difficult combination in a dog.

Keeshonds are not easy to train unless, perhaps, they have a very good relationship with their owner. They are very inclined to bite back when corrected. If this happens, they should be punished very severely. If it gets quite out of hand, I would suggest the dog be put down.

Airedales I've had rather limited experience with, so I can't comment — other than to say that those I have trained needed a very firm hand.

Rough Collies are very gentle, and, being obedient by nature, don't usually need to be trained. If you wish to train your Collie for pleasure, however, go slowly, giving your dog virtually no physical correction and ample praise. He'll obey more to earn his praise than to avoid corrections, which often confuse him. Remember that a Rough Collie is unlikely to co-operate with someone he doesn't care for. He will work only for someone to whom he is attached. Even an expert will get little change from a Rough Collie that doesn't belong to him.

Schipperkes, provided they're well built and sturdy, make excellent pupils.

Poodles are clever enough to train — and then again, clever enough not to if they don't want to! If they enjoy their lessons they'll learn with ease, but the average amateur will have little luck unless he has a very sturdy little dog and is exceptionally patient with him. Be careful, however, not to frighten your Poodle, or you may ruin his temperament for life.

Staffordshire Bull Terriers are sensitive dogs and like to please their owners. Although they're a little on the short side, they're not difficult to train. They make affectionate and charming pets — apart from the fact that they like to please, their coat doesn't need much care, they don't yap, and they don't get out of hand if they miss a walk.

Most Staffordshire Bull Terriers are fighters and this trait is virtually impossible to cure, unless you start teaching them to get on with other dogs when they're pups. But should another dog attack your Staff, his latent fighting instincts will probably be roused — and he'll die fighting rather than give it up! (See chapter 3 for separating a dog fight, and the last chapter for dealing with fighter dogs.)

English Bull Terriers have courage — and a resistance to correction that is unbelievable. I always feel when I've trained a Bull Terrier that he's obeying with his tongue in his cheek! He isn't a dog that merely obeys his owner's command. He 'makes a decision' before he does so! If, however, he's devoted to his trainer and is trained with the approach suggested for dogs in category (5) above, he can train extremely well. Brown Bull Terriers are generally less stubborn and strong-willed than white. Like Staffordshires, they're fighters, and you won't change them.

Beagles and *Corgis*, if they're to be trained, usually need the assistance of the tips given to the owners of dogs in category (5). And it's not unknown for a Beagle to have a touch of the brain-power described in category (6). If you want to train your Beagle — show him who's boss, and don't give up — because he's hoping you will!

Because Beagles were so recently kept mostly in packs,

most of them have retained their interest in other dogs that often exceeds their interest in people. And because he is a hunter, his highly developed scent organs pick up distant scents—and off he roams to investigate.

A *Bulldog* shouldn't be trained, because his breathing passages are too restricted to allow him to exert himself. And, *because* he can't exert himself, he doesn't usually need training!

Spaniels (including Cavalier King Charles Spaniels) know perfectly well what they were bred for—hunting. Oh, to follow a trail—*any* trail—and, ironically, the more you let them go the easier you will get them back. Then the desire to chase a scent becomes less pent up, and he pays *you* more attention. Domestication often places too heavy a demand on a dog with much love of the hills and dales—or even just next-door's dustbin.

Spaniels can be trained to make them more manageable, but they don't, as a rule, adapt very well to a regular training programme. Spaniels usually have a deceptively high threshold of correction. In fact, you could almost go as far as to say that once a Spaniel has made up his mind on some small matter, such as, for instance, who is going to rule the household, there's precious little you can do about it!

Bassets, in spite of their build, can train more easily than you may expect. Their reactions are very slow, and they can be extremely stubborn, but once they see that you mean business, they'll oblige—usually with a bad grace! Unless they enjoy their lessons, training shouldn't be a regular sport with Bassets; they have heavy bodies and short legs, and heel work is often a bit much for them, especially when they're competing against dogs of the same weight, but with two or three times the length of limb to carry them!

The habit they have of teasing their trainer can leave some Basset owners somewhat nonplussed, but if they're in need of training a few lessons should make them more manageable around the house. Don't be misled by his lack of stature—he's a big dog, and needs the space and exercise of a big dog!

Being a hunting dog, like the Beagle described above, his highly developed scent organs are inclined to pick up distant scents, making him roam far and wide.

There are the individual dogs amongst the other smaller breeds that, with the right owner, will train extremely well. Generally speaking, Terriers need a firm hand, and toys need gentle handling.

5. *A dog to breed from*

The subject of breeding dogs is dealt with in full in chapter 4. In that chapter, we come to the conclusion that if you want to buy a dog to breed to make a little pocket money, you'll be lucky if you come out even—and if you *do* make, it's *hard* work!

If you're wanting a male dog to put out to stud—the bitches won't beat a path to your front door unless he's got a few red letters behind his name, and to make a dog a champion involves an expensive pup (or a bit of luck!), a lot of know-how, trips to all the dog shows, and lots of patience.

6. *A companion for your other dog*

If you're seeking another dog because yours is lonely, consider perhaps, whether he doesn't want more of *your* company, rather than to be made to share it. If this can't be remedied, you may have two lonely dogs rather than one.

People mean more to dogs than they do to each other. Dogs in kennels may romp and play and curl up together but as soon as a person comes into sight they gaze longingly through the wire.

However, this is not to say that dogs do not need canine company. They certainly do need to mix with other dogs from time to time.

(At this point, it would be as well to note that control over one dog is far easier than control over two or more. A reflex is precipitated in a dog by hysteria, the excitement of another dog, and so on. This is known as pack behaviour. The dog is then no longer under the control of his owner and two dogs form the nucleus of a pack.)

If you feel you have the time for the demands of an extra dog, and yours won't be jealous of another pup in the house, get him a companion preferably of the opposite sex. But if you feel your dog is likely to be jealous, but needs a playmate, the ideal set-up is a friendly dog from the neighbourhood to visit occasionally—but not all neighbours are as friendly as their dogs, so this can have its drawbacks! You may even consider getting him a kitten to play with. Dogs can form very strong attachments with cats.

If your dog is already getting on in years, but still

enjoys life, a playful pup may well rejuvenate him. But if he's old, a new pup will make him miserable, with his constant demands and playfulness.

7. *A dog to replace your previous pet*

If you lost your dog through some accident—whether on the road or at home—you will, of course, not expose the newcomer to the same dangers. Your garden will now be fenced off, inoculations attended to and so on.

The desire to replace a dead pet completely is often the main motivating factor with some people when they're buying a pup. Going back to the same breeding kennel, and seeking a relative or a dog with exact markings, and then continually watching for similar characteristics in the new pup only lead to disappointment. It's best not to try to resurrect a beloved pet, but to accept that he's now at peace, and enjoy the experience of a totally new dog. If you're disappointed that he doesn't live up to the standards of your other dog, remember it's not *his* fault that he doesn't cock his leg the way old George used to—a dog must be appreciated for his own personality: like wine, he'll improve with age.

If, however, you're considering buying a new pup before the old one dies, so that when he does go you won't feel quite so bad, give the old boy some consideration. After a lifetime of devotion to you, he deserves better than to have to endure the attentions of a youngster continually worrying him for a game just when he needs sleep and peace. And having had you to himself for so long, being made to share the love that has always been his, will make his last few years or months a misery.

If you're replacing a pet that had to be put down because of viciousness, nervousness, insanity, or some other hereditary ailment, don't buy another from the same kennel, and check with his pedigree (if he had one), avoiding any dog that has close relatives in common with your previous pet.

45

(c) The Choice of a Dog to Suit your Temperament

A tall beer-drinking, back-slapping, joke-telling fellow who owns a gentle and sensitive Collie will, unwittingly, make his dog's life a misery. If Grannie owns a young Boxer, *her* dog will also quite unwittingly make *her* life a misery.

... beer-drinking, back-slapping, joke-telling fellow ...

A family with four healthy, noisy young children, playing cowboys and Indians and having disagreements and spankings from time to time, who own a soft-natured Poodle, may adore their dog—but *he* is going to be an often unhappy and frightened little animal.

Before you choose your breed *and* your dog, look at yourself. If you're short of stature and softly spoken, the best breeds for you are *Dalmatians, Rough Collies, Setters, Greyhounds, Whippets, Schipperkes, Toy Poodles* (which incidentally, together with *Miniature Poodles*, are the most suitable dogs for people who are allergic to fur—provided the dog is clipped and brushed regularly to keep it free of dust) and most toy breeds.

Beagles, Boxers, Bull Mastiffs, Bull Terriers and *Dobermans* are, as a rule, too strong-willed for you. *Bassets, Scotties, Great Danes, Keeshonds, Border Collies, Corgis, Sealyhams* and *Spaniels* are also often rather strong-willed as well. Lastly, one finds both tractable *and* strong-willed dogs amongst *Golden Retrievers, Ridgebacks* (the lighter built dogs of this breed are easier to handle than the heavier ones), *Fox Terriers* (the wire-haired variety are usually more stubborn, lively and strong-willed than the smooth-haired) and other breeds. Even the often sporty and always affectionate little *Poodle* frequently needs a firm hand.

When choosing a pup, a softly-spoken person should ask the advice of the breeder and watch the litter at play—choosing a pup that gets the rough end of the bullying.

Poodles, Spaniels, Collies, Greyhounds and dogs that are highly strung, including most of the toy breeds, however, shouldn't go to homes where the family is excitable, especially where they have loud voices which are high-pitched or raised. This will cause a lot of problems with the dog. Placid dogs settle down better in an excitable family.

Also, if you aren't a person with too much patience, don't choose a breed of dog that requires the careful grooming necessary with some breeds. Grooming a woolly dog, a *Poodle, Spaniel,* or *Afghan,* for example, is a task that needs lots of patience.

If, however, you're a firm, decisive sort of person, you should choose a dog that you'll respect and enjoy. When the cheeky blighter in the litter who bullies all the others grows up, *you'll* be able to handle him!

It isn't entirely a dog's training that determines how

obedient he is, but also the strength of character of the person who's handling him. If, for instance, the wife in a particular family can manage the dog, but the dog ignores her husband, you can bet hubby's hen-pecked! Just as a social structure was set up in the litter, so it is in the home—with either husband or wife at the top— or the dog. (Perhaps that's what they mean when they say 'top-dog'.)

Before you choose your breed look at yourself

If the various members of the family are assorted personality-types, an average dog that'll suit them all is easily found. The extremes mentioned above don't occur all that often—but often enough, and cause a lot of unhappiness when they do.

(d) **The Choice of a Healthy Dog**

Once you've chosen your breed, look at several litters before you finally select your pet. Try to choose a pup that's round, plump, glossy, playful and reared in clean surroundings.

Although you don't want to be landed with a pup that's sick and weak—a visit or two to the vet can cure any small ailment the dog of your choice may have—first and foremost get the dog with the right temperament.

Don't consider buying a pup that's reared under filthy, neglected conditions. Such 'breeders' should be brought to the notice of your local animal welfare organization.

Your pup will bring you far more pleasure if he is used to being gently handled by people. Dogs are believed to go through a critical period when they are between three and six weeks old and unless they form a satisfactory relationship with people at this point it is believed that they never will.

Your pup should be eating by himself when you take him from his mother. If he's removed from her *and* put on to solids all at the same time, the break may be too much for him, and he may not have the confidence he would otherwise have had.

If you're buying your pup from a breeder who lives some distance away, try, if possible, to fetch him yourself. It's not unusual for buyers to be misled when buying a pup they've never seen. Also, the journey may be frightening for the pup and the experience could affect him for the rest of his life.

Try to ensure that both parents are good-natured,

being neither vicious nor nervous, because both these failings are usually hereditary. If, however, the mother appears a little vicious when you approach her puppies, make allowance for the fact that she's probably guarding them. Seeing her on her own will help you decide.

It's wise to find out if the breed you're interested in is prone to any hereditary disease. Some white dogs (*Bull Terriers* in particular, for instance) are prone to deafness, some strains of *Golden Retrievers* and *Collies* to blindness, and *German Shepherds*, *Labradors*, *Golden Retrievers* and one or two other breeds are prone to hip dysplasia.

Deafness can be detected while a litter is asleep. A noise will waken them, and unless a deaf pup is disturbed by the movement of his brothers and sisters, he will continue to sleep in spite of any loud noise. Blindness and hip dysplasia, on the other hand, don't usually manifest themselves until the dog is older, and only a certificate from a vet, stating that both parents are free from either of these diseases, can assure you of a pup that comes from parents free of these ailments—but it's an expensive procedure to get the dogs X-rayed and examined, and, unfortunately, not all breeders are prepared to do it.

If your enquiries lead you to a breeder that is reputed for not breeding from any dogs carrying hereditary diseases, you should certainly try to buy a pup from him.

(e) Pedigreed or Mongrel?

Those who argue in favour of a pedigreed dog say they *know* what they're getting, and take a pride in the breed of their choice. Those who argue in favour of mongrels say they're hardier and have more personality. Even if I wanted to, I couldn't persuade either group of dog-fanciers to think otherwise.

However, where I do disagree—and with vast

Pedigreed or mongrel?

experience with dogs to back me in my opinion—is with those who say pedigreed dogs have a superior mentality to cross-bred and mongrel dogs. Just because a mongrel doesn't have all his ancestors looking the same, with their names written down, is no reason why he should have less charm, less intelligence and less value attached to his life. Admittedly pedigreed dogs *are*, to a greater or lesser extent, selectively bred, but what for—their charm and intelligence? Or the shape of their head and the length of their tail? A superior temperament is limited neither to a pedigreed nor to a mongrel dog. The choice of either is purely a matter for personal preference.

If you are buying a pedigreed dog and you want him purely as a pet—you may save yourself a bit of money if you tell the breeder that you are prepared to pay a lower price for a dog that has some show fault, rather than pay a higher price for a dog that can compete in the show ring.

But be sure you want the dog *only* as a pet. If he's not registered and properly transferred into your name (see later) it's too late to decide you want to show him when he's fully grown!

These faults are not faults in the dog's temperament, and don't matter in any way other than that they are points of difference where nature and the judges don't agree—like uneven eye colouring, 'wrong' ear carriage, 'wrongly' shaped teeth and so on.

When you buy a pedigreed dog, ask for your pedigree certificate *with* your pup. Don't be put off with promises that it's lost, or will be sent on later, because it so often isn't! Moreover, you want to get a dog from a breeder who cares about the dogs he is breeding. There are many breeders who are breeding from poor stock, and

even faking pedigrees. All too many people find out too late that their pedigree is not in order, or worse, that their dog is lame.

The breeder should supply you with: a pedigree certificate reflecting three generations of the pup's ancestors; an original certificate of registration in the name of the breeder; and transfer forms.

When you buy a pedigreed dog, unless his pedigree is registered at the Kennel Club, the dog cannot be shown, nor can any of its puppies be registered. If a dog is to be registered, *both* his parents must be registered.

1. *The Kennel Club*

The Kennel Club regulates dog shows. No official dog shows, or obedience, working or field trials, may be held without the licence of the Club. It classifies breeds and holds the records of all breed standards, adjusting and amending where necessary. It keeps records of affiliated kennel clubs and training clubs, approves Championship Show judges and keeps stud books and records of champions, and issues the *Kennel Gazette*—a dog magazine with all up-to-date information about pedigreed dogs, and matters pertaining to registrations and affiliated clubs.

Under present regulations the breeder must register the litter. Unless this is done, the dog cannot be later put on the Active Register, a necessary formality before showing and breeding. The breeder will register the pups with or without a kennel name, and with a common name. This name remains with the dog for the rest of his life, and cannot be changed—except for the addition of a suffix, which may be added *only* at the time of transfer.

The prefix in the kennel name reflects who bred the dog; the common name differentiates him from other pups the breeder has bred; and the suffix, if any, reflects who bought the dog. The kennel name may be registered or unregistered, and if you don't add your own suffix on the transfer forms at the time you buy your pup, you cannot do it at a later stage.

If the dog you buy has a registered kennel name, the breeder is more likely to be proud of the quality of the dogs he is breeding, because the name is always there, and a glance at his pedigree shows who bred him.

A kennel name cannot be the name of an area, a breed, a town, an adjective, a colour, a number, and so on. It must have a personal meaning for its owner—a family name, a house name, or a name made up from a combination of the names in the family, for instance.

Say the kennel name chosen by the breeders is Timbridge. If the breeder wishes to register this name with the Kennel Club, he will apply for forms—and must supply the alternatives requested on the forms, should someone else already have the kennel name he has chosen. No two people can give their dogs the same kennel name. (These alternatives are important because it causes the Club a great deal of extra correspondence when they are omitted. *Typed*-out forms also save it a lot of headaches.)

Right, so his kennel name is duly registered as Timbridge, and then his dog has, say, three pups. So he registers them as, for instance, Timbridge's Rover, Timbridge's Pluto and Timbridge's Fido. Along comes Mr Jones and buys Timbridge's Rover. He fills in the transfer forms which the breeder has obtained from the Kennel Club, and duly signed over in his favour. (In fact Mr Jones *typed* them out!) And then he adds his own suffix, Blackbeard, for instance. This, he sends off with the fee. Now his dog has the legal status of bearing the name of 'Timbridge's Rover of Blackbeard'.

But when he wants to call his dog he doesn't shout 'Timbridge's Rover Blackbeard, heel!' because by that time Timbridge's Rover will be around the next corner! The dog doesn't even need to be told of his fancy kennel name, and the Kennel Club doesn't need to know his nickname, which he will come to answer to—Fifi, Peter, or whatever.

2. *What is a pedigree?*

A pedigree certificate is a list of the names of at least three generations of the pedigreed dog's ancestors. If it's a pet pedigree, it will be an indiscriminate list of pedigreed dogs of the same breed obtained from reasonably accessible sources. If it's a pedigree belonging to a dog that's bred for showing, it is likely to have the same names or kennel names appearing several times over, because these blood-lines have certain desirable qualities their owners are seeking to bring out in their litters.

A dog with a pet pedigree can certainly become a champion dog, although he can't be depended on to produce champion pups—however good the bitch he mates. This is because his pups may take after Uncle Rover who had a squint eye, or Cousin Jim who has bandy legs. (Technically speaking, he has too varied an assortment of recessive genes.) On the other hand, inbred dogs of average quality that have outstanding ancestors may well produce champion pups, because they're not carrying such an assortment of recessive genes. There will, therefore, be no throwback—unless it's a throwback to a champion, which is what his owners will be hoping for.

A pedigree certificate means very little, unless the reader knows what each dog written on it looks like and what kind of puppies he or she is producing. However, most of us who own an expensive pedigreed dog are delighted with any red names (champions) there may be written on it—and why not?

(f) **Male or Female?**

A male dog doesn't have puppies and a female dog doesn't cock a leg around the place, or wander off in search of romance (not quite as much as a male dog does anyway). A female dog, once spayed and the bill paid, has no breeding problems. Male dogs are always in demand, so I needn't sing their praises. I think you just 'pays your money and takes your choice'!

(g) **Puppy or Adult Dog?**

I'm sure I don't need to list the advantages and otherwise of owning a puppy. Everyone knows the fun these inquisitive little bundles of fluff and mischief bring—and the work and inconvenience involved: puddles on the carpet, squealing at night, missing slippers, and chewed possessions.

. . . puddles on the carpet . . .

Buying an adult dog on the other hand is often approached with some misgivings. 'Will the dog transfer his affection to us?' or 'Does a dog have to form attachments at an early age if he's to be completely loyal to his owners?' are some of the questions asked by people before embarking on buying a fully-grown dog.

If, firstly, you don't want to be bothered with puppy-nonsense, secondly, you want your watch-dog immediately; and, thirdly, you want to see what your dog's temperament is like, your only course is to buy an adult dog.

. . . and chewed possessions

Your new dog should, with patience and love, transfer his loyalty from his previous owner to you in a surprisingly short time. If, however, he does pine and refuses to eat for more than a week or so, he should be returned to his previous owner. If this isn't possible, and the circumstances force him to be parted from his owner, he should rather be put down. Not many dogs refuse to accept a new master, but it does happen occasionally.

If you're thinking of changing his name, do this when he's settled down; he won't take long to accept a new one. (You cannot, however, change the name on his pedigree. If no suffix has yet been added, you can add your own, but if his previous owners added theirs, then no further change can be made.)

You can judge a dog's age only roughly. His teeth are sharp until he's about four months old, and at about three years old they may start discolouring (their teeth).

A pup starts losing his milk teeth at about four months of age. He has 28 milk teeth and 42 permanent ones.

A large dog has loose-fitting skin until he's about nine months old. A large dog's paws also give away his age until he's fully grown—he usually looks as if he has one size too big for him, until he's about nine to eighteen months old, depending on his breed. And, lastly, you can judge whether or not a dog is fully mature (seven to nine months in small dogs, ten to twelve months in large dogs and eighteen to twenty-four months in the giant breeds) by the strength of their legs. Until this age they sway slightly when they walk, and it only takes a gentle push—and they're over on their backs. An adult dog has strong, firm legs and, if he's a male and doesn't cock one yet, he's still a pup.

Ask whether or not your new dog has had his inoculations. If he has, you should get the certificate in case of kennelling and so on.

In Britain a young pup does not require a licence but a licence must be held for all dogs of six months of age or more. You can obtain one over the counter at your Post Office.

And of course, if you're paying the price of a pedigreed dog, you want the pedigree certificate right away. If, for any reason you can't be supplied with the certificate when you make payment, the chances are that he's not pedigreed.

Try to ensure that you're not having a problem dog palmed off on to you. It would be wise, also, to enquire whether he can be returned within a week, should he prove to be unsuitable.

An adult dog may try to run away during the first few days after his arrival. Put your own phone number on to his collar as soon as you get him, and keep him closely guarded until you're confident that he won't try to get away. A dog that's frantic to escape may get through, over or under almost any window, gate or fence. Be particularly careful if he just sits quietly, making no apparent effort to escape. He's just thinking.

A dog that finds himself suddenly in completely strange surroundings may like something familiar in his new home—a favourite toy or his own bedding, for example. For a while give him the food he's been used to (or something extra special), and ask what games he likes to play.

It's not wise for the dog's previous owners to visit him, especially shortly after his move. He will become confused and his loyalty will be divided. A dog never forgets owners he was once attached to.

A favourite toy

CHAPTER 2

PUPPY DISCIPLINE

(or how not to have a problem dog)

What is Puppy Discipline?

Your pup cannot move into your home and do just as he pleases. And you, on the other hand, won't find that *your* life will continue in the same way as it did before he arrived! You will each have to make certain adjustments, and 'puppy discipline' is that point where your pup must adjust and fit in with your life—and yet not have demands made on him which deny him his right to live 'a dog's life'!

A dog is a dog, with the needs of a dog, and this entails certain adjustments on your side—but he is now a family member, and must be trained so that he becomes a pleasure, and not a burden on the family.

'Puppy discipline' is that balance where you teach your dog to restrain some of his natural instincts, and rechannel certain of his abilities—yet *still* allow him to be a dog. He must release his excess energy, meet other dogs, have opportunities to find new scents, have companionship and express his personality. He's not a person. He won't wipe his feet on the mat, or bark only whenever it suits *you*. Nor is he a vegetable—he can't sit all day and do nothing. But he is a *dog*, and he's capable of going a long way in meeting you half-way— that is, being disciplined.

Owner-discipline is dealt with here and there at later stages in the book—where you'll least expect it!

Tone of Voice

You cannot communicate effectively with your dog if you don't use the correct tone of voice when you give his commands or when you speak to him.

If, with people, *our* tone of voice conveys more than the words we speak . . . how much more does it with dogs! Be confident and positive and clearly differentiate between command, reproof and praise.

Correction and Reward

Your pup was disciplined by his mother as soon as he started crawling around. She made it a very pleasant experience for him to be a good puppy by giving him a loving lick and a close snuggle, and she made it unpleasant for him to be naughty by shaking or nipping him to check him.

You can continue the good work nature has started by adapting this early training to your own form of reward and punishment for him. The reward he gets is the same—only *he* does the licking and *you* do the snuggling! When he obeys you, show him that he's been good by petting him, telling him he's good, picking him up and displaying the utmost delight.

You may be tempted on occasions to reward your pup with a titbit rather than with praise. But you want him to obey to please *you*, not himself. Don't underestimate your pup—he's capable of nobler motives than obeying just to satisfy his animal appetites. Don't underestimate yourself—he can still love and want to please you, even if your pockets *are* empty—and why teach him cupboard-love when he's born innocent of it?

And if he isn't hungry or has a tummy-ache, what then? But his appetite for praise he never loses.

Punishment is different for each dog and circumstance. When you first get your pup he's tiny, and a tap with your forefinger is the strongest correction he should get. As he gets *older* (and naughtier) your punishment may have to becomes more severe. If you find he's devastated by a sharp word—punish him simply with a reprimand. You should never use any physical form of punishment on this type of dog, he'll make a devoted and obedient pet if raised with patience and kindness. But most pups are lively, curious, bold and resilient little creatures. They'll need some form of correction that's more effective than a scolding.

If his punishment is to be an effective deterrent to disobedient behaviour, it must be worth avoiding.

If your pup squeals when he's smacked on his rump, you need use no stronger measures. But if he thinks it's a game, or tries to dodge you next time, don't be afraid to hold him by the loose skin on each side of his neck and give him a good shaking.

Smacking a dog on his nose may possibly make him flinch when you put your hand near him in the future. If you over-correct him it definitely will, but if you find that it's the only correction he heeds, he'll gain confidence again as he becomes more obedient, thereby getting less punishment and more rewards. If you stroke his face gently when you reward him, this will also help him stop flinching. Chapter 1 discusses several breeds, and the section on choosing a dog to train will help you decide how heavy a correction your particular dog is likely to need.

Some people use a rolled-up newspaper to correct their dog. You may not always have your newspaper handy just when you need it, but your hand is always there! You can over-correct a timid pup, and under-correct a bold pup with a newspaper, but you can adjust your corrections accurately with your hand.

To repeatedly under-correct a lively and mischievous pup is fatal—he's bound to become crafty and calculating; you can just see his little mind working: 'Can *I nip Puss and get away with it*? Even if I do get a whack, it'll be a small price to pay—it's worth it!' But if he knows he'll get a really good whacking, he'll dismiss the idea as not worth taking a chance on.

Always make it up to your pup the instant you've punished him. Contrary to what you may expect, it will in no way diminish the effect of your punishment, but it will prevent him from becoming scared of you, *and* from developing independent ways.

When you find you have to correct your pup for doing something he's not allowed to do, like biting a cat, chasing chickens or jumping on furniture, always keep the temptation in front of him for a moment afterwards. Then he can show you he's learnt and is resisting the urge to repeat his misdemeanour—whereupon you will, of course, reward him. This will make the lesson twice as effective.

You may, at some stage, catch Pup red-handed doing something that's forbidden—stretching himself out in comfort on the best Chesterfield suite, for instance. If, the moment you appear, he quickly hops off, looking very uneasy, and you say to yourself, 'Oh, well, at least he *knows* he's not supposed to', he'll think: 'Good, I got away with it—I must just be more careful not to be

. . . red-handed . . .

caught next time!' Punish him, however guilty and ashamed he looks, before he becomes a confirmed offender. However, don't let a chase develop. If he's indoors when you find him, close the door before you correct him so that he can't escape. If a hunting match develops, he'll either develop a keen sense of sport and become incorrigible, or he'll become terrified.

A relationship of two opponents must not at any stage replace a relationship of a master and his dog.

If Pup is allowed to get away with his crimes repeatedly, he'll get out of hand. Behaviour that's cute when he's small may be a real problem when he's fully grown. Always punish your pup the very first time he shows signs of biting and the moment he starts chasing cars, cats or chickens. Don't hope he'll get over it, he won't — he'll get worse.

Punishing a dog is, I am afraid, essential. (I am, of course, referring more to the average spirited dog than to willing or timid dogs.) *Not* punishing him is cruel. If your dog were still wild, his pack leader would be busy making him and the rest of the young ones in the pack submissive. So follow nature's course and make him submissive. If he does as he pleases — sending everything in his path flying, running wild on a walk, biting, fighting, digging, chasing and chewing — so that no one will be able to tolerate him, *he'll* suffer for it. So be kind to him and rechannel these high spirits into a desire to please you, and make him a happy, well-behaved and much-loved dog.

You may find with a lively and spirited young dog, however, that no matter how much you punish him he still continues to commit his crimes. It may not be that you are under-correcting him, but that you are expecting too much of him. A golden rule to follow, whatever you are trying to teach your dog is: meet his need, and then punish his greed. If you don't meet his need, he will fight through any punishment, however severe. This may be whether he is needing more exercise, needing more attention, or if he's stealing food when he's hungry — or whatever the circumstance may be.

Always meet his need, so that he doesn't resist his corrections, then, if necessary, punish his greed, so that his demands do not become excessive.

It may also be necessary for children to know how to manage a dog if he jumps up against them, knocks them over, licks their faces and takes their biscuits. Parents of small children often ask me how they should teach their children to cope. This is a difficult question to answer, because it depends on the age and temperament of the child. If a child is inclined to be a bully, not only is he probably capable of defending himself against his dog, but telling him to punish his dog isn't going to be good for him. On the other hand, you can help a gentle, timid child to fend for himself and gain confidence by teaching him how to handle a rough dog. The child's mother must decide whether to correct the dog herself, or whether to show her child how to.

To conclude: respond to your dog, and he will respond to you. The more you give, the more you will get back. Meet his *need* for love, attention and so on—and punish his greed for too much!

House-training

This entails a couple of weeks' inconvenience, watching the pup, and having lots of newspapers handy.

While your pup is very tiny, it'll be easier to train him on to newspaper—his sense of direction is still a little primitive and he'll never find his way to the front door at critical moments.

To help your pup to start using newspaper, let him sleep in a fairly large cardboard carton at night. Divide this into two sections—his bedding on one side and newspaper on the other. You'll find that he'll always do his business on the paper when he wakes up. (Be careful, however, that the paper is changed regularly. He won't like using dirty paper—so he'll go and soil his bed.) This will get him used to using newspaper, and he'll be more likely to go to it when he sees it on the floor.

If you're concerned about your carpets, confine your pup to the kitchen until he either learns to look for newspaper to use or is fully house-trained. It's reassuring to know that, should Pup puddle on your carpet, no mark will be left if you sponge it and then put a dash of soda water on the spot. Then add pepper, so that he doesn't get ideas next time he goes there.

When he's old enough to find his way outside on his own, lift him up gently each time he wakens, has finished playing, or sniffs about in a suspicious manner. (Don't startle him, or he'll forget what he was about.) Take him to a spot in your garden where you'd like him to soil in future and stay with him until he performs—whereupon you tell him he's a good boy. He may understand better what he's been taken outside for if you put down a piece of newspaper—particularly if it's been used.

When Pup puddles inside for the first couple of weeks, regard his mistakes as your own, because he's still small and is still learning, and he hasn't much control over his bladder.

Dogs like to do their business away from where they sleep. You'll get quicker results if you take your pup to a distant spot in the garden. (When he's older, take him for a walk.) If you just put him out of doors in the evening, and then ten minutes later let him in again, sure as anything he'll wait at the door until it's opened again—and do what he was meant to on the kitchen floor at a later stage during the night.

If you'd like him to 'do his thing' on command, say 'Grass-grass' (or anything you choose to say to him, as long as it's always the same) each time while he's performing—then reward him afterwards. You'll be grateful for this when, in the middle of winter, you want to get him inside quick—and he obliges on command.

After a couple of weeks, when you feel that he should know better than to mess indoors while he has access to the garden, scold him if you actually *see* him misbehaving. While he's still small, he won't understand if you punish him some time after he's done it.

If he still continues to misbehave after another week or two, smack his bottom. Nothing more severe than this is necessary at this stage. He should not, of course, be kept indoors for such long stretches that he can't help himself. If he repeatedly goes to the same spot to soil inside, this is *his* idea of how he's being house-trained! At least you're making *some* progress! Put pepper on as suggested, and be more watchful.

It'll be some time before he's able to go the whole night without relieving himself. No dog likes messing inside once he's house-trained, so put a piece of newspaper at the door (some distance from his bed) and he'll use that, rather than the floor.

If you live in a flat, follow the same procedure, but teach him to go where you've decided you'd like him to — on a sand-tray, or a pile of newspaper, or whatever arrangement you have for him.

House-soiling in an adult dog is dealt with in the chapter on problem dogs, which also has a few tips that may help you with house-training your pup.

Coming when Called

To teach your pup to come when he's called, you should, firstly, never call him when you're powerless to enforce your command. It's an easy mistake to make and we all make it. It teaches a pup that he needn't take commands seriously. If at any time he's doing something you don't like, and the circumstances don't permit you to take action (or you're feeling too lazy to get up), ignore him.

However, if you're anxious that he should come to you, but you're powerless to enforce your command, lie flat, make funny noises or run the other way—or all three! Or pretend to talk to the cat, and you'll stand a good chance that his puppy curiosity will bring him.

But don't trick him too often, or he'll get wise to it.

or talk to the cat . . .

Never punish your dog when he does come to you—however long he took, or however naughty he's been. This has a devastating effect on a dog's trust. If you do want to punish your pup for running away, or for taking too long to come to you when you call him, or for committing any crimes on his way to you—you can't. He'll interpret it as being administered for *coming* to you—when he eventually does.

To teach your pup to come when he's called, call him for his food, a game or a cuddle, thereby setting up pleasant associations with coming to you. Sit on the floor, pat your thighs and call him brightly. Don't call him when he's too preoccupied (no point in deliberately putting yourself at a disadvantage), enjoying himself too much, too often, or for anything unpleasant. He'll start thinking the whole business of being obedient is too demanding. When he comes, let him climb on your lap and tell him now marvellous he is, always making it worth his while to come.

Never grab your pup, because that will teach him in future to keep just out of reach. It's such an easy mistake to make—and it's maddening! If your pup is a little nervous, or reluctant to come to you, sit or crouch down, keep your hands on your lap, say 'good dog' warmly and lovingly—he won't be able to resist it, and in half a second he'll be on your lap!

Even if you're in a hurry, *never* grab him! Always *tempt* him to you with the proximity of your face and the warmth in your voice.

If, however, you need your pup to come to you for something he's not going to like, rather than make *him* come to *you* for it, go and fetch him. Or, call him and make such a big fuss of him for some few moments that he feels that *that's* what he came for!

Follow these rules until he's ready for formal training, then, if necessary, round him off with the help of chapter 10 when he's mature.

Teaching a Pup to Stay Quietly on His Own

Your pup must get used to staying alone on occasions, without voicing his displeasure—assuming, of course, that he does get adequate company and isn't just plain lonely.

If, when he is left by himself, he begins to bewail his fate loudly, barge into the room and tell him very sharply to 'Quiet!' (or cruder language).

How fearfully you thrust yourself upon him, how sharply you speak, and whether you need bang a table or not, depend on his temperament and his age. Without experiencing utter terror, he must draw back for it to be effective—otherwise your presence will be most welcome and he'll squeal again for your return.

As you see him draw back, close the door *immediately*. If you hesitate to see if he's heeded your reprimand, he'll gather courage to start squealing again. Close the door instantly, and he'll settle down.

He'll be far happier snoozing with the knowledge that you won't come to his rescue, than anxiously hoping you will—and getting a sore throat and ulcers in the process. And you've laid foundations for commanding him to stop barking at a later stage in his life.

Chewing Household Effects

If your pup starts teething on furniture, shoes and carpets, he'll do irreparable damage. Give him a shaking and a piece of your mind. If he's tough, point to the damaged object and smack him on his nose once or twice. Then put him in his basket with a marrow bone to teethe on. If there's a possiblity that he's chewing out of boredom, rectify that as well.

Picking up Dirt

Puppies are inquisitive little creatures, so they'll eat all sorts of dirt. This generally leads them into no trouble—in fact it's nature's way of building up their resistance to illness. If a dog never comes into contact with dirt while he's a pup, he'll fall ill at the first sign of a germ when he grows up. More harm is done making them nervous by fussing.

However, don't leave sharp bones or poison lying around where he can get at them, and his puppy curiosity won't get him into any serious trouble. The section on first aid, page 155 will tell you what to do if your dog does swallow something and looks ill, trying to vomit and refusing to eat.

Playing Gently

Your pup has needle-sharp teeth and he doesn't realize that you don't have the tough hide his brothers and sisters had to withstand them. If he bites in play, say 'Gentle' or 'No' sharply, and smack his nose. If he's a 'chewy' dog, give him a stick to chew on, or a rag to tug while he's playing with you or while you pet him.

However, if he snarls at you, or bites in earnest, make it very clear on the spot that he has very wrong ideas about who's boss in the house. Lift him on each side of his neck so that you're face to face, and he's dangling helplessly—and give him a lecture he won't forget in a hurry. Shake him, put him down, and make friends again.

Jumping Up

When your pup is tiny he's picked up—when he gets bigger, he misses the proximity of your face, and jumps up to get closer.

To teach your dog not to jump up, step towards him as he leaps against you and correct him (as described below). At the same time, say: 'Don't jump!' very sharply. Then pet him lovingly, insisting on all four feet on the ground. This is as important as the correction.

Correct your dog by thrusting your knee sharply into his chest. If he dodges your knee, catch his front feet while you say 'Don't jump!' and, holding his legs up, thump him. Then pet him as described above. Don't give a thought to breaking his spirit or anything like that. A strong dog that hurls himself against you, and then uses his wits to dodge all your efforts to prevent him, won't get his spirit broken in a hurry.

As you take your hands away from him after petting him, say: 'That's enough!' If he jumps up again, repeat your command and punishment. Then step back, and, bending over, holding your hands out towards him, call

him to you—*with your hands accessible to him*. And
repeat your 'Don't jump!' command. It's essential that
you bend over and make your hands accessible to him,
or he will certainly jump up to seek them—they must be
there for him to come to. Pet him for not jumping, then
say 'That's enough!' again as you take your hands away.

If you are not a strong person, and have a large, lively,
young dog, thumping him in the chest with your knee
may be a little awkward for you. You will, I am afraid,

have to hit him. You won't like it, I'm sure, but if you're to live together amicably your dog will have to learn to respect you. He is a tough dog, or he wouldn't be displaying this exuberance.

If your dog is small, follow the 'Don't jump!' routine but, to correct him, merely tap his nose, and instead of bending over you can just pick him up to pet him. When you put him down again, repeat: 'Don't jump!'

To recap

As your dog jumps up:
  (1) Step forward.
  (2) Point your finger.
  (3) Command 'Don't jump!'
  (4) Punish.
  (5) Pet your dog.
  (6) Step back with hands accessible to your dog.
  (7) Call gently so as not to excite him.
  (8) Tell him not to jump and correct him if necessary.
  (9) Pet and reward him.
  (10) Command 'That's enough!' to dismiss or calm him.

Don't say 'Down!' to your dog if you intend to train him when he's older, or he'll confuse his commands.

Remember: Meet his *need* for your greeting and petting. Punish his *greed*. If you don't meet his need, he'll fight through his punishment and become incorrigible. If you don't punish his greed, he'll ask for more than you have either the time or the inclination to give him.

As he learns, he'll run to greet you, hesitating before he jumps up against you. You must instantly put your hands down for him, or, sure as anything, up he'll jump—and we can't blame the dog then, can we?

To help curb your dog's high spirits, give him your full attention for about a minute when you return home after an outing. *Match the intensity of his greeting* (a tall order, no doubt, but he'll be less demanding afterwards if you do), using both hands to pet him. After a minute or so, switch him off by saying sharply 'That's enough!', making it quite clear that he's had enough attention for the moment, and instead of following you around, hang-dog and hopeful, he'll look for a bone to chew or go and have a nap.

If he jumps up on your visitors, either ask them to give him a quick greeting, or do so yourself, then dismiss him as described above, if necessary out of the room, until he's trained.

(The chapter on problem dogs deals with jumping up in adult dogs.)

Stolen Loot

When your pup steals your new slipper, don't give chase. You won't catch him, he'll enjoy it, and tempers will be lost.

Impossible and crazy as it seems—fuming like a steam-engine, with one sock on and a bus to catch—sit on the floor near him . . . and relax. Say lovingly and convincingly to him *'There's* a good little chap!' (which he isn't). You can even swear at him, as long as you do it lovingly.

He'll find the proximity of your face and the promise in your voice irresistible and—provided you don't move towards him or display any impatience—you'll soon see how quickly he forgets about the sock, and sidles up to you as if he's done nothing wrong. But don't grab him, or the smart little devil won't come close enough next time you want something from him. Just give him the caresses you promised in your voice, and stealthily recover your stolen object. (I know I don't have to say—control your urge to skin him alive when he does come.) He'll grow out of these thieving ways, and punishing him will make it much more difficult for you to get your possessions back next time—and if next time it is your knitting that's unravelling with every step he takes. . . .

When he's older, tap his nose and command him to 'Leave!' until he voluntarily surrenders his loot, and gets a warm reward. Look upon it as one of the inconveniences you asked for when you bought a puppy; it's only mischief not a crime, and the phase doesn't last long.

'Outside!'—'Basket!'—'Off the Garden!'

There'll be occasions when you want to dismiss your pup from the room. Start teaching him to go out on command when he's about four months old.

To teach him 'Out!', point to the door and command him very firmly—your attitude leaving him in no doubt that you mean it, even if he has to be put out bodily.

No chase must develop—be subtle, and command him only when you know you have the advantage of a strategic position over him. Anticipate his dodging manoeuvres and see that you win every (or nearly every) round.

When he begins to understand what's required of him—he'll do his utmost to avoid going out. So, don't send him out too often and be very firm and, within a few weeks, a strict expression, coupled with a pointed finger, will leave him in no doubt that the wisest course of action is to go, and he'll realize that it does not, after all, mean eternal banishment.

After he's learnt to go out on command, follow the same procedure for 'Basket!', or whatever he sleeps in.

To teach your pup not to walk over your flower-beds say fiercely, 'Off the garden!' the very first time he ever sets foot on your daffodil bulbs. If he's a tough dog give him a shaking. It may take some weeks to get the message through, but if you're persistent he'll learn.

Sit and Shake Hands

Your pup can be taught to sit and give a paw as early as eight or nine weeks old. It's most impressive to see such a little thing being so clever!

This early teaching develops a dog's capacity to learn and please. Also, it's easier to teach a pup to sit than it is to teach an adult dog that has strong back legs to resist you with.

Push your dog down gently, saying 'Sit!' firmly but kindly. When you have made him sit, reward him profusely. Repeat this a few times each day.

After a week or two, if he's not already obliging you with a response, give him a little tap with your fingers on his bottom after your sit command. Then praise him extravagantly as he tucks his little backside in to escape the impact of your fingers. He is still very tiny, so be very patient, and don't upset him in any way.

Continue with this as he grows up, and by the time he's fully mature he'll be sitting readily in preparation for his training programme—and for everyday convenience.

While you're teaching your pup to sit, ask him for a paw, take it and show pleasure. After a few times, see if he volunteers his paw, eager to get the praise he knows will follow. If he doesn't, repeat your request, touching his paw lightly to prompt him. (This is one of the rare occasions where you *ask* a dog—not *command* him.) With plenty of patience, and not too frequent sessions, he may delight you with a loving look and a tentatively outstretched paw.

If your pup can't catch on to what you're asking him to do, don't let it bother you.

Lie down!

Start teaching your pup to lie down when you tell him to, when he's about three or four months old. This is not the 'Down!' command, but a firm request to your dog that he lie down at your feet, on his mat, or under his favourite chair when you have visitors, and so on.

Because he is still young, his legs are floppy, and it's easy to push him over into the lying position. Tell him 'Jason, lie down!' firmly but kindly, flop him over, pat him on his shoulder, and tell him he's a good dog. (Dogs don't like a hearty pat on their head!)

He'll get up straight away, but do it a couple of times a day and, after a few days, hold a pointed finger and tell him firmly to stay there—pushing him down again if he gets up.

As he gets older, tell him in a firmer tone to lie down and pat the ground in front of him to show him your intentions. Be firm, relaxed and patient. If you have an excitable dog, don't reward him, but if he's not an excitable dog you can show him your approval with a pat and then hold up a warning finger to show him he must still stay down.

Don't make your dog lie down too often; be firm about it and, if possible, show your approval when he obeys.

Getting a Pup used to the Lead

When your pup is quite used to you and his new surroundings, let him get used to his lead before he becomes too strong or, in the case of smaller breeds, too stubborn.

Put the lead on him from time to time in the garden. When he begins to associate the lead with outings, he'll become eager to wear it.

If your pup is very nervous and panics when he feels it on him, get a *very* light lead. Pick your pup up (don't let him see the lead), pet him and talk lovingly to him. While you're doing this, let someone put the lead on him carefully so that he doesn't notice. Pet him further and put him on the ground and let him walk *to* something. Perhaps just one step to a piece of bully-beef, or something equally tasty, or a friend can hold the lead so that he can walk to you, and then you make a big fuss of him; or he may like to run to an open car door.

Start off by letting him walk a step or two, and *gradually* increase the distance, over the days or weeks, until he no longer minds being attached to the lead—because on it, he goes to something he eagerly anticipates.

Don't let him walk too far at first, and don't let him feel the restraint of the lead. He shouldn't even be aware of it at first. Whatever he runs to—he must run *eagerly*. Always chat to him, pat him, trot along with him—let it be *fun* to walk on the lead!

Do this every day, and if you have no success, wait until he's about nine months old. If he still refuses a lead, the section in the chapter on problem dogs will help you to encourage him to accept it when he's mature.

When your dog is used to his lead, let him wear it on occasions, so that he doesn't lose his willingness to wear it when comes the time that you need to use it, or want to start training him.

Always let your dog enjoy the scents he picks up on his walk, and restrain him as little as possible. (Dogs that take their owners for a walk are sorted out in the chapter on problem dogs.)

Precautions against Poisoning

You can't teach a dog to detect poison in a piece of meat. The other alternative is to teach him to refuse to take food from anyone but yourself. Firstly, I think this is a little beyond the average dog's understanding, and secondly, it means that you can't be separated from him at any time in his life—or he starves. The procedure is to find a friend who'll give your dog a piece of meat and then punish him for taking it. It's bewildering for the dog, and can well break down his trust in people.

To teach your dog not to pick up food lying around may be a bit more humane, but when he's learnt, knowing dogs as I do, I'd say that if he finds a morsel, he'll look first left, then right, and, seeing no owner, will sneak off to eat it where no one can find him.

Poisoning *can* be a problem, and if you're afraid of your dog being poisoned—rather keep a better watch on him.

Road Sense

Many dogs roam the streets carefully, looking left and right for cars before they cross. It's doubtful whether their owners actually took them out as pups and instilled the highway code into them before allowing them out on their own. It's more likely that they weren't properly confined in their homes, used their wits to escape being run over, and those that didn't get killed learnt to handle traffic.

Admittedly, guide dogs are taught to find their way about in traffic with superb efficiency, but not all the dogs that enter guide dog schools pass with flying colours. The dogs that ultimately graduate have exceptional ability and are trained over long periods by very skilled handlers, with the correct equipment. Even then they are trained to provide information for the blind person but only to cross on command.

Putting up a fence is easier and less frustrating. Dogs should not be allowed to roam free. In built-up areas they create a growing anti-dog lobby on hygiene grounds. They are in danger of getting injured or run over and an even greater hazard to traffic trying to avoid them. Even in country districts they can be a nuisance, harrying livestock. Your dog does not have to be a sheep-killer to create havoc if allowed to roam uncontrolled. Let your dog have all the exercise it needs but let it be on your own territory or outside under supervision. If you are not prepared to do that do not keep a dog.

Conclusion

Your pup must grow up with inhibitions about doing as he pleases. He has an intelligent and adaptable mind, and (in most cases) a resilient body.

However, don't bend him too far. We are disciplining our dogs to adjust to our mode of life—but we, too, must make certain adjustments. A dog must give expression to his personality, have an outlet for his energy, and a *reason* to obey.

A dog must give expression to his personality

Your dog should be rewarded for every command he obeys (how profusely you reward him depends on how much he gave up to obey you) and punished for every command he disobeys.

Do not command him any more than is necessary.

Maintain as high a standard of consistency as possible —what is wrong today is wrong tomorrow.

Lastly, the two attitudes that enable you to control a lively dog are:

(1) a loving, warm and intimate attitude; and
(2) an authoritative and masterful attitude. (Not to be confused with a domineering attitude, which never brings a dog security or happiness.)

When your dog is disobedient and excitable, the combination of these two attitudes correctly applied quickly brings him under control. Despair, frustration, anger, lukewarm commands, and so on, are neither — and make him worse.

As your dog becomes more obedient, you will automatically reduce the amount of authority you had to show while he's young and boisterous.

Correction and reward in the adult dog are discussed in chapter 7, and when your pup gets older this chapter will guide you further.

CHAPTER 3

CARE OF YOUR DOG

(a) General

1. *Pup's first night home*

When you bring your pup home, he's going to be miserable at first when he finds he now has to sleep all alone. You, too, will be miserable when your hear his pitiful wailing in the night!

The best thing to do with a confident young pup is to give him a run and a game as late as possible so that he can relieve himself—and get nice and tired! Check that he does his business before bringing him in and then put him in a bed that he can't get out of. The warmth of a hot-water bottle will be comforting for him, but wrap it up securely in a towel so that it neither burns him while it's hot nor chills him in the morning. The muffled ticking of a clock should have a soothing effect on him — assuming of course, that the alarm's turned off! You could also leave a fluffy toy in his bed for him to curl up with.

He's sure to cry for you, but sooner or later he'll settle down and go to sleep (probably later than sooner!). It's kinder to leave him, because if you keep returning to him he'll keep expecting you and won't settle down to sleep very easily. He'll need to spend a penny when he wakes up, so take him outside first thing in the morning.

However, if your new pup is timid and afraid, don't leave him alone at night until he's gained a bit more confidence. Resign yourself to the fact that you have a sleepless night or two ahead of you, put his bed next to yours, and give him reassurance in the night. A highly strung pup like this will only get more hysterical as the night wears on if he's left alone. When he knows you well, then make new sleeping arrangements.

2. *Bedding*

Because a pup no longer has the warmth of his mother and litter-mates, his bed should be warm and comfortable. If he sleeps indoors, he can't get stolen, and he's not likely to wander off in the night and get lost.

A youngster with busy jaws usually makes short work of wicker baskets, which you can give him when he's finished teething—and when you're better able to judge his full-grown size. A cardboard carton is easily obtained, and can be replaced when it gets chewed up. A piece of foam rubber covered with a couple of ironing blankets are cheap and make a snug bed. Dogs seem to have forgotten the hardship and discomfort their ancestors endured—and love their luxury. Your pup will appreciate a comfortable bed.

You can cut a door in one side of his carton for the first few days, so that he can go in and out when he feels like it during the day, and while he's still tiny you can put the open side against a wall at night so that he doesn't wander around and get lost. When he is older, you can discard his old carton and give him a wicker basket. These are comfortable for a dog, supporting him all around his back, while he sleeps. They are also easy to keep clean. The basket shouldn't be too small for your dog—he should have enough space to sleep comfortably.

A pup loves his bed, so during the day it should be accessible to him to retreat to when he needs a nap, or a little peace. All through his life he should have his own little corner for his bed, in an out-of-the-way place (preferably not next to a stove where he can get burnt). He'll like it, and *you'll* like it when he's not on the carpet or at your feet all the time. His bed should always be dry and not in a draught.

If you are giving your dog a kennel, see to it that it doesn't get the wind or the rain in it, and that it is always dry and quite weatherproof.

And, lastly, no dog should sleep directly on concrete. This absorbs all the warmth from the part of his body that is lying on it, and as the dog gets older he will become prone to rheumatism and arthritis.

3. *Naming your pup*

If you give your pup a name that carries with impact when you call him, you'll be able to teach him more easily to come when he's called—and it'll make it easier for him to pick out his name when he's spoken to (or about).

When you choose his name, remember he won't always be a puppy. Some names may be cute on a little dog, but if he's going to be a big dog give him a name that will also suit him when he's fully grown.

4. *Handling*

Until Pup has settled in and gained confidence, children shouldn't make too many demands on him. Shouting and playing roughly around him may confuse him until he's used to his new surroundings. And while he's still tiny, he shouldn't be played with for too long because he'll get tired.

A pup needs lots of sleep

The relationship between pups and young children is discussed further in chapter 1, in the section on choosing a dog for a companion.

When you lift your pup, support him properly. His mother may have picked him up by his loose skin, but now he's too heavy and he won't like it.

When you want to pick up your pup, rather than try to catch him, let *him* come to *you*. Children should also learn this. Put yourself in his place, you're more than ten times his size, and a child scampering after him can be terrifying for him. Go near your pup, sit on the floor, and talk invitingly to him, letting him come all the way up to you. If you reach out and grab him, he'll learn to dodge your hands, and soon he'll be able to run faster than you! If he's hesitant, a second or two more patience will bring him to you. If your pup's a little nervous, keep your hands right in and speak to him in low tones to 'draw' him right up to you, keeping quite relaxed—and only touch him when he's come right up to you.

If he's asleep when you want to pick him up, he shouldn't be woken unless it's necessary. If your pup *has* to be woken, stroke him first so that you don't startle him.

If your pup isn't the only canine member of the family, and he has a big brother or sister that looks upon his arrival without quite the same enthusiasm as you do, include *him* in your displays of affection over the new arrival. If you do this, they'll accept one another more easily, and in no time will be good pals.

5. *Routine*

Because a puppy is a baby, he needs his routine. His little tum can only take in small amounts of food—so he must have his three meals a day. And because he's a baby, he needs plenty of sleep if he's to grow strong and healthy.

An adult dog also likes a routine of walks and meals at regular hours. He comes to look forward to these highlights in his day, and is happier if he can anticipate them and depend on them. He does, after all, get only one meal a day—and when it's due, he's hungry.

6. *Collars*

When your pup is about three months old, put a collar on him with his name, your phone number and/or your address on it. In Britain it is a legal requirement for a dog to carry some form of identification. His collar must never fit him tightly, and because he grows so fast you'll have to check to see if it needs adjusting or to be replaced from time to time, until he's fully grown. A leather collar should fit an adult dog so that your hand can slide under it with ease.

If, when you put the collar on your pup, he fusses and scratches at it, take him out for a game, and he won't give it another thought.

If your dog wears a check chain, this should also fit him correctly. When it's drawn closely against his neck, about 5 centimetres should protrude from the loop. This is then comfortable for him, he can't get his foot hooked in it, and it can't slide off his head, or get hooked in his mouth.

If you live in a farming area, however, it's not a good idea to put a check chain on your dog, because a link in the chain can get caught on a piece of barbed wire when he's out exploring and climbing under fences. This happens easily, and there he struggles until he's rescued. In fact, it is never a good idea to leave a check chain on an unsupervised dog. Even at home they can get a claw or a tooth caught in a link.

In some areas, dog thieves are prevalent. A big dog wearing a leather collar can resist being taken by force by sliding free, whereas a dog wearing a check chain cannot.

A glance at the lost column of the newspaper will convince you of the necessity of putting your phone number or your address on your dog's collar. You may both live to be eternally grateful that you went to this little bit of trouble!

There are various ways of doing this. The easiest and surest, if you live in one of the main cities, is to go to a pet shop or a chain-store which will supply and engrave a disc for you while you wait.

You can also buy a Dymo label maker from a stationery shop and stamp your details on to this. (It is a little costly, but can still be useful for schoolbooks, sunglasses, and so on, afterwards.) But the label will come off the collar unless it's glued on securely with a good brand of glue. While the glue is drying, clothes-pegs can hold it in place for 24 hours.

A marking pen can also be used, but the wording will have to be renewed from time to time.

Lastly, small barrel-like containers for particulars are available. They are particularly useful if you regularly take the dog to stay with you at a second home—you simply change the slip of paper inside for the one with the local address—but they sometimes fall open within a very short time and the details are then lost.

7. *Safety*

If your garden is fenced before your pup arrives, and your gates are kept closed, he won't get lost or run over. Some people with a garden that has a single gate leading out on to a busy road put a spring on the gate. Messengers and forgetful children are so often the cause of a dog being let out and run over when the gate is inadvertently left open.

When you drive your car on your driveway, don't expect Pup to get out of the way on his own. He's too small to anticipate the direction of an approaching vehicle and unnecessary heartbreak can occur by expecting him to. A car also provides shade in summer, and the warm engine attracts pets in winter. It's a good idea to acquire the habit of looking under it every time before you drive off.

Another danger to dogs is sharp bones. Chop, fish, chicken and rabbit bones all splinter and can puncture a dog's intestines. These bones should never be given to dogs.

Electric cords are another potential source of danger to a chewy puppy. If he's left in a room to his own devices, he may well try to teethe on a cord. If it's plugged in, he's in danger of being electrocuted. (If this does happen, never touch the dog until the current is switched off and the plug pulled out. A dog may urinate when he's electrocuted, so be careful not to stand in any puddle he may be lying in, as this will also be alive with current.)

Not many households leave poison lying around, but a dog can be unwittingly poisoned. If, for instance, the room where you've placed your pup's food and water is sprayed with insecticide spray, the residue will settle on his water or his food.

Your pup can also be poisoned if he's sleeping in a room which has just been sprayed, or eats a rat or grasshopper which has been poisoned.

Snail pellets in the garden can also be a danger to a curious little puppy that likes to have a taste of almost everything he sees.

8. *Jackets*

A recently chipped poodle, or a dog with a sparse coat, like a Dachshund, may well appreciate the extra warmth of a jacket during cold weather. A dog that shivers while it is sleeping is not just shivering from excitement and may be cold. Keep an eye on the dog for parasites if it is worn for any length of time and remove it when the weather warms up.

9. *Companionship*

A small puppy should never be taken into a new home where he's left alone for long hours. The contrast between the play and bustle of life in the litter and a large, empty, silent and lonely house will make him very unhappy, and a pup cannot develop his full potential of intelligence, confidence, and personality if he's left alone for long hours.

A dog's place is in the home with his owners, rather than out of doors all day. A dog that spends his life outside, alone for most of the day, either becomes mentally stagnant, overwhelmingly exuberant or independent of his owners, amusing himself by chasing cars, digging, pulling down the washing from the line (great fun when it's flapping in the wind!), roaming, and so on. When a young dog is confined outside in a yard, he becomes lonely and bored, spending a lot of his time listening for footsteps at the door and building up tension . . . and when he finally sees his beloved mistress come out, basketful of clean washing under her arm, he flings himself at her in sheer delight, releasing all his pent-up energy all over her, and making up for lost time. The washing goes flying into the mud, the dog—thoroughly enjoying being the centre of attention for the moment—gets shouted at. And no one dares to go outside again.

Sometimes a dog is confined out of doors, simply because when he's let in he just goes beserk all over the house. However, when he's got over the first ecstasies of being allowed to share the paradise of his owner's home, he won't be nearly so wild, especially if he's disciplined and trained. Show him authority—not anger. Clout him—don't shout at him! And, of course, give him some attention.

The section on over-exuberance in the chapter on problem dogs will help you further on how to cope with him.

And, lastly, an outdoor dog doesn't develop the same feeling of protectiveness towards his home as does the dog that, living close to his family, feels he belongs with them.

There are those who go to work and *have* to leave their dog alone all day. Such people really should not keep a dog—and if you know that a dog will have to be left alone do not buy one. Of course, our circumstances change and you may find you have to leave a pet you already own. You will have to fit his exercise and other needs into your free time and hope that he can adjust more easily to the enforced loneliness with time.

If the dog is allowed in the front garden where he can see a bit of activity he'll be happier, and a few bones to chew will also help to pass the time for him. You can also feed him in the morning, so that he'll probably sleep when you leave him. With his tummy full, he won't feel quite so lonely when he's left alone. But what so often happens is that when he's been sleeping all day he's full of life when his owners come home—too tired for the games and attention he's now wanting!

10. *Play*

Having been taken from his mother and brothers and sisters who played with him every day, your pup will now expect *you* to be his new playmate! If you have two pups, you're relieved of this duty, though you'll doubtless find it difficult to resist wasting hours playing with both! Playing is important to a dog. It keeps him healthy and alert and maintains his youthful spirits. A notice in a toy-shop window says, 'Play and stay young'. This certainly applies to dogs as well.

To encourage a pup to play on his own, a piece of old tyre, sack or rope hanging from the branch of a tree will give him (or them) hours of fun and healthy exercise—and his owners lots of amusement.

Whenever you give your pup a toy—let it be big enough so that he doesn't go and swallow it!

Tug of war is also a favourite game with some dogs. It's supposed to help loosen their first set of teeth when permanent ones are pushing through.

Lots of dogs adore retrieving, and this keeps them very fit. Once a dedicated retriever, always a dedicated retriever! When children throw objects for dogs they must take care because the dog doesn't—he'll chase a ball under a car or over a precipice in his excitement.

If, when your dog gets old, he still chases balls madly, don't let him get too tired. He probably won't know when to stop, and it will strain his heart if he overdoes it.

Because pups swallow stones and small objects pretty frequently, it's better to play with objects he can't swallow—balls, and sticks, never stones, for instance.

If you avoid teasing or annoying your dog when you play with him, you won't make him irritable and bad-tempered.

11. *Outings and exercise*

Dogs that lead an oversheltered life and never go out often grow up into nervous dogs. They are not to know that the world doesn't end at their boundaries, and when they see lorries, crowds, traffic and big dogs for the first time they're terrified—particularly if they live in a walled-in garden.

A pup should be introduced to crowds and traffic gradually so as not to overwhelm him. This way, he'll develop into a confident adult dog.

When you take your pup out, don't protect him unless you have to. If a dog comes over to say 'Hullo!' with his tail wagging and with obviously peaceful intentions, and you pick your pup up, he isn't to know he hasn't been snatched from the very jaws of death!

However, until two weeks after your dog's inoculations, he shouldn't be taken out, because of the risk of infection.

Long walks are tiring for a pup until he's mature, but a fully-grown dog needs his exercise. Without it a young adult dog will become destructive and out of hand and, when he's older, fat and lazy. Well-exercised dogs develop a nice gloss on their coats, and, like people who get plenty of exercise, have fewer medical expenses and live longer.

A fully-grown dog needs a regular run with fresh smells and complete freedom. Consider the muscles and energy of a large dog and see him move with power and speed, and then wonder why he jumps fences, chews furniture, digs gardens and chases cars when he's confined and denied a rightful outlet to his energy.

And small dogs? Well, look at the pleasure they get from a chat and a 'top 'n tail' with a neighbour, a trot in the park and oodles of sniffing at glorious scents. Their sight is said to be colourless, but so are our noses! Just as *we* don't like to be denied aesthetic pleasures, nor do *they* wish to be denied their odorous equivalent! Scents mean a lot to a dog—to them it's like getting all the latest news and gossip every day!

Problem dogs that are brought to me seldom get completely sorted out until they are taken for a regular free run. It can be a problem for busy housewives to find the time, but sometimes their children enjoy a visit to the park or the beach, or, if the children are still young, a ride in the pram, as much as the dog does his walk. Sometimes Mother begins to lose weight, or Dad takes up jogging! Whatever the circumstances, they almost invariably report that the outings are enjoyable.

However, like people, when a dog gets out of condition, trying to make up the exercise that he's missed during the week will strain him and do him more harm than good.

A word of warning here—it's not wise to let children exercise a dog unless there's no traffic in the area. A child has not the same control over a dog as an adult has, and I've known a number run over this way. Not only is the dog injured or killed, but it's very distressing for the child.

While you're walking your dog in a built-up area, or even along a country road, do not let your dog off the lead. If off the lead in open country, train him to wait for you at any road and re-attach his lead. If you let him cross the road alone, he may get run over while trying to run back to you when a car is approaching. This can be avoided by keeping an eye on him and seeing that he doesn't cross the road without you.

Where there's no safe place for a dog to run free, he can be fastened on to a rope a little longer than the conventional short lead to give him more freedom. But be careful with a big dog not to get whipped off your feet if he runs around you and then hives off full tilt in another direction!

When walking in busy city streets, don't let even the most obedient dog off his lead. The unexpected can always occur and the dog can be startled into the road, or lose his owner in a crowd.

When you're exercising your dog, don't worry about inclement weather—neither rain or cold will hurt him. However, it's not wise to let a dog go from the hot fireside out into the freezing cold, or go to bed wet after a walk in the rain in the evening. And if he gets very wet after a walk in the rain, towel him down before the heater or fire before he goes to bed.

Fighting

If your dog is a fighter, exercising him off the lead does present a problem, unless you have an area near by which is free of other dogs. Muzzles are not completely effective because dogs just fight through them.

Although there are not too many hardened fighters around, there may be an occasional dog that will attack a pet out on a walk. If you're not a strong person, it's a good idea to have a stick with you on these outings. This doesn't mean, of course, that you should lash out at every dog that comes near yours! It's reasonably easy to tell when a dog's going to fight. He lowers his head and advances in a very threatening manner. If an unknown dog's intentions are peaceful, however, he usually holds his head high, with his ears slightly back, and walks with a sort of stiff-legged trot. His hair may stand up on his back but this doesn't necessarily mean he's angry.

Should there be a dog-fight, your stick, unless handled skilfully, shouldn't be used to try to separate the dogs—it will only make them fight more furiously. Pepper doesn't touch them, and water's also useless—it only refreshes them. A strike aimed at the aggressor's back legs *may* be painful enough to make him release his victim and look around to see what hit him, and the dogs can then be snatched apart in that split second; or, if the aggressor is wearing a collar, a long stick can be placed through it and twisted until he begins to choke and is forced to let go.

If there's someone around to help you, each can take a hind leg (preferably by the thigh) or a tail, and sooner or later (probably later than sooner) the dogs will release their grasp and they can be pulled apart. If the dogs can be lifted off the ground by their back legs they'll let go sooner when suspended in the middle.

If I have to separate two large dogs alone, I swing the aggressor in the air, causing the victim to land through a doorway, or over a fence. There's usually some convenient spot near by where you can drag the fighting dogs to—the strength comes from somewhere when you need it!

Small dogs, or dogs of average size, can be separated easily. Lift the aggressor by his scruff in one hand, and take a handful of skin or a tail in the other, and shake him until he releases his victim. Hold his scruff as close to his head as you can, so that he can't turn around and bite you.

At all times when separating a dog-fight, keep your hands well away from the dogs' faces, or you're likely to get bitten. Your dog won't bite you intentionally, but he'll think he has hold of a piece of his opponent.

Dogs usually recover pretty quickly from a dog-fight— unless its a small dog that's been attacked by a big dog.

However, most dogs are willing to be friendly with one another. Many fights are actually caused by the dogs' owners. When they're having a tentative sniff, hair prickling and tails taut (the dogs', that is), they're ready to defend, should the other attack. But if their owners step towards them, they usually interpret this advance as encouragement (or are eager to defend their beloved owner from a potential source of danger). Perhaps someone shouts 'Dog fight!' and each dog in this moment of commotion thinks he's about to be attacked by the other dog—and therefore fight. If you see your dog stiff-tailed and menacing, encircling another, say lightly, 'Come boy', turn your back, pat your side and walk away. If you think there's going to be a dog-fight, it is the *only* way you can prevent it. Your dog will quickly follow, eager not to be left behind.

A dog is most likely to attack when: another dog is trespassing on his property or coming near an owner or young; when one dog is a hardened fighter or has become hardened as a result of teasing or through having been previously attacked; and, finally, when dog owners panic and precipitate a fight. Throwing a stone, shouting, touching the dogs, or even just speaking to them or stepping towards them can cause them to fight while they're just summing each other up.

When you take your dog out in your car, rather than let him lean out of the window let him sniff the air from one that is slightly open. More than one dog has enjoyed leaning out so much that he was never seen again!

Teach your dog to sit quietly in the car, and also teach him not to jump out as soon as the door is opened. It's easy for a dog to get run over if, as soon as the door is opened, he jumps out into a busy street. When you're taking him out of the car, place his lead on him before you open the door. And if he's safely locked up when you leave him in the car, he cannot, of course, get stolen.

It's not uncommon for dogs, when left in closed-up cars, to get heat-stroke. This can be avoided if, firstly, your dog can get fresh air from an open window (but not wide enough for him to jump out and get lost or run over) and, secondly, the car is parked in the shade. Check also, that the sun is not likely to move over on to your car before your return. On a hot day the temperature in a car, left in the sun for as little as twenty minutes can reach 60°C (140°F). A dog would get heat-stroke and die long before the temperature got anywhere near as high as that—to say nothing of the distress he would suffer in the meantime. When you go shopping on a hot day it's better, if possible, to leave your dog at home.

If you're taking your dog on a picnic, to the beach, or on a shopping outing, he'll appreciate a drink of water. A dog gets very thirsty in a short while in the heat, his cooling system depending on the evaporation of water from his tongue. A good idea is to keep a Tupperware dish both for carrying his water in, and for him to drink out of.

A dog that gets car-sick can usually be cured if he's taken on a short ride each day until he no longer gets sick. After each ride let him have something to look forward to—a run, or a game, for instance. The length of the ride can gradually be increased—first simply down the driveway, then down the road, later around the block, and so on. The eagerness with which he will come to anticipate his game or run should help him to overcome his car-sickness.

Don't feed your dog for some hours before his journey, and take newspaper with you to put on your car seats.

If he looks a little 'green about the gills' during the ride, stop and let him get some fresh air. If he messes your seats, don't, of course, be cross with him for it!

Green about the gills . . .

When your dog is used to the car, take him out from time to time, so that he remains used to it.

Should you need to take him on a long car journey before he's used to car-rides, your vet can give him motion sickness tablets. Also, stop from time to time to help prevent his getting sick.

Lastly, on your way home, after any outing, a quick check that Rover *did* pile into the car with the rest of the family, and he won't get lost!

Getting lost

If you're afraid your dog may run away when he reaches an open space while you're out on a walk, don't pursue him. The chances are, that as long as he knows you're behind him, he'll have the confidence to go further. But, when he notices you're no longer in sight, he'll probably sniff his way back to you, just as scared of losing you as you are of losing him! If you've let him out of your car well away from other traffic, just start the engine and drive a little way—he'll be right there in no time, asking to be let in! But make sure he's not hiding underneath it first. In general it is better to only let him out of the car on his lead and take it off when well away from roads.

Should you at any time lose control of your dog in busy traffic, never call, shout or chase him, or you'll increase his fear and drive him under the wheels of a passing car. Simply crouch down and speak lovingly to him, and when he spots you or hears your voice, he'll run to you for refuge. Don't stand up or attempt to catch him until he comes right up to you. When he comes, first pat him and reassure him, then lift him, or put his lead on him.

If you ever lose your dog, notify the police station, and your local sanctuary immediately and put an advertisement in the 'lost' column of your local newspaper. Many dogs are reunited with their owners in this way.

You may, on the other hand, see a dog that you think may be lost and would like to try to restore him to his owner via the same media of newspaper, animal sanctuary or police station. You can usually tell whether a dog is lost or not by the way he walks. If he walks with a purpose in his trot, leave him—he knows what business he's about. But if he looks scared, glancing this way and that, or is hungrily searching for food (unless he's the local fat slob scrounging around dust-bins!) he's probably lost. If he's afraid, the procedure described above in getting your frightened pet to come to you, and in the section on nervousness in the chapter on problem dogs for approaching a frightened dog, may help, but you may have more difficulty with a strange dog. If you're successful in securing the dog, guard him closely or he may try to run away before you can return him to his owners. If you're unable to win his confidence, rather than risk frightening him into the traffic, report him to your local animal sanctuary.

Swimming

Some dogs enjoy a swim, and it's very good exercise for them.

Dogs should not, of course, drink sea water. The beach can get very hot, and there's very little shade, so remember to pack his water in with your coke and tea!

If there's no shade available, an old dog shouldn't spend any length of time on a beach in the hot sun.

Take care with a small dog when he's swimming, as he can be carried away by a current if he swims out of his depth in a river or the sea.

It's not all dogs that enjoy swimming, however, and if you'd like your dog to swim but he's scared of the water introduce him to it gradually with the help of a few games. If he still won't take to it, he's best left—it's not serious. The more frightened he gets, the less likely it is that he will ever learn to swim.

A dog shouldn't swim with a loose-fitting check chain, as his foot can get caught in it and he can drown.

Some dogs are allergic to the salt or chlorine in the water—the best cure for this is to hose them down after a swim.

(b) Grooming

An unsightly and smelly dog cannot give the same amount of pleasure as one that's kept clean and well groomed. The amount of grooming he'll need depends on his breed (or mixture thereof). If he's of a breed that needs special attention, consult a book, or the people you bought him from, for advice on the care of his coat.

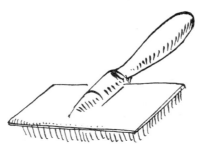

1. *Brushing and clipping*

All dogs benefit from an occasional brushing. Your dog won't shed as much hair in your house and odour-forming bacteria are removed.

Always be careful when you brush your dog not to hurt him. Some dogs have coats that get badly tangled — *Poodles, Afghans, Pekingese, Old English Sheepdogs* and *Spaniels*, for example. If you don't have the time or the patience to get the tangles out, rather let a good parlour attend to it for you. But if you allow a dog's coat to get like this, even with the best care, it's painful for him when he's brushed out. It also causes his hair to break and makes his coat look dull. To avoid this happening, these dogs should be gently combed or brushed out every couple of days—daily is ideal of course, if you have the time for it.

The best type of brush to use is one like that shown in the illustration. Tease tangles out gently with a metal comb—or cut them off. The brush and the comb can be obtained from a pet shop.

Sometimes dogs seem to shed their hair interminably—however much you brush them! If your dog has short hair, a flea comb will help get rid of a lot of his loose hair. If he has long hair, try grooming him with a wet brush—and a piece of sticky tape rubbed over clothing and furniture will quickly pick up any hairs he's shed where he shouldn't have.

Your dog may be losing his hair because he's out of condition. Refer to the chapter on first aid to help you restore his coat to condition, and give it a nice healthy gloss again.

Dogs usually moult and get their new coat at the change of season in March and September, or, in the case of bitches, three months after they've been on heat. Unless dogs are groomed every day while they are moulting, it is very difficult to get rid of all their loose hair.

If your dog's coat requires professional attention, don't send him to just any parlour. Some insist on keeping the dogs all day so that they don't get an opportunity to relieve themselves, and also spend long hours waiting for their owners quite unnecessarily. Others are very rough, and the dogs hate their visits with the pain and fright they involve. A parlour that lets you look around before you send your dog is obviously proud of the way they handle dogs.

Some parlours have driers, which frighten many dogs. To save your dog this—and yourself the extra pennies— you may like to bath him yourself the day before his visit. If your dog's hair is tangled, however, either get (or cut) the knots out before you bath him or leave it to the parlour, otherwise his coat will become matted. However, some parlours will automatically bath a dog and will insist on doing so.

If there's a sudden drop in the temperature when your dog is due to be clipped, leave it a while—if the temperature is likely to warm up. In midwinter you can ask the parlour to do only his feet and face, or not to clip him too short, otherwise the little shorn thing will shiver with the loss of his coat! But if you're allowing his coat to grow longer for the cooler weather, it'll need to be brushed out every day, or it'll give him blazes when next he goes to the parlour.

If, on the other hand, the weather's very hot, he may like to be clipped a little sooner than he's due, and he can enjoy feeling cool again.

Some breeds must keep their long hair if they are to be shown and their owners point out that they do not have any problems in seeing their way around, but I feel that a dog's hair shouldn't grow into his eyes. I do not believe that he can see properly, and this may make him nervous and bad tempered. It's a common fallacy that a dog that has hair growing over his face has weak eyes and needs the hair to filter the light.

The characteristics of some breeds have become exaggerated by man's selective breeding. *Poodles* and *Spaniels*, for example, have ears that have become pendulous and hairy, preventing adequate ventilation around the ear canal. Their ears become clogged with dirt and bacteria, causing a condition generally known as canker. This condition can be prevented by removing the hair that grows inside the ear passage—this your vet or parlour can do for you, or show you how to.

Lastly, the hair around your dog's feet; if this is kept trim, he'll bring less dirt into your house.

2. *Bathing your Dog*

How often should a dog be bathed? Experts on dog care vary in their opinions from once a week to never.

When I'm asked how often a dog should be bathed, I feel it depends on the breed, and your circumstances. Woolly dogs, such as *Poodles*, need to be bathed every two to six weeks, depending on whether you live in a dusty area, whether you want to show your dog, whether he's white or black, and so on. Other long-haired breeds, such as *Alsatians*, need to be bathed every two or three months—depending on how often they're brushed—or they get smelly, the dirt and bacteria irritate them, and they start scratching.

No dog, however, should be bathed more than once every two weeks.

If you bath your dog frequently, and he is completely without fleas, you can use either a specially prepared dog shampoo, which you can buy from a pet parlour or pet shop. Or, equally effective, use one of your own shampoos for dry hair. Olive oil in the rinsing water will also help prevent a dog's coat from drying out.

A dog that has fleas should be bathed with an insecticidal shampoo. An ordinary shampoo doesn't kill fleas.

. . . use a special shampoo

There are reputable insecticidal dog shampoos that do. They do not have a strong odour, do not dry out the dog's coat, and will clean him and rid him of the fleas.

If your dog is small, pop him in a tub. If he's large, he can be washed in a sunny spot on the lawn. A dog that won't co-operate when he's being washed can be fastened to a post with a check chain and lead. Win his confidence by soothing him, and then be very firm with him while you wash him. Pour a bucket of warm water over him, let it soak well into his coat, shampoo him, then rinse him down with a hose. Be careful not to get soap in his eyes. A drop of water in his ears is soon shaken out—but his ears must not be washed out.

If, as soon as he sees he's clean, he goes straight into the dirt and does something about it—which, given half a chance, he'll do—the dirt will brush out when he's dry and, believe it or not, his coat will still shine. However, you should only let him dry out like this on a very hot sunny day. Otherwise he needs a good rub down with a towel. Make sure he's really dry and he will lose the urge to roll in the dust.

If you wash your dog's bedding as well as your dog, he won't start smelling all over again the next day.

If your dog is rather smelly and is needing a bath, but for the moment a bath is inconvenient, you can brush his hair upwards and sprinkle a little medicated baby powder in his coat.

3. *Nail clipping and teeth care*

Some dogs never need to have their nails trimmed, while others' grow long, needing attention if they're not to cause the dog discomfort.

A dog's nails have a quick which contains nerve endings and blood vessels. If this is cut, it's painful for him. If he has transparent nails, the quick is easily seen (especially with a light behind it) and can be avoided, but if the nails are black, it takes an experienced person to clip them without hurting the dog.

A dog's teeth also need attention from time to time. If they become caked with tartar, his gums become inflamed and his teeth then become loose and fall out. This doesn't happen so easily to dogs that get food they can chew. A meaty shin bone once or twice a week will help keep a dog's teeth clean. If your dog's teeth become caked with tartar, the vet can scrape it off for you. When you take your dog to the vet, you can ask him to take a look at your dog's teeth and nails. A pet parlour can also clip his nails for you.

4. *Parasite Control.* (See page 143).

(c) Diet

1. *Water*

Fresh, cool water in a clean bowl should always be easily accessible to your dog. Dogs don't enjoy drinking stale water.

Every day you drink a cool drink, or tea, coffee, and so on, and unless your dog has his water-dish filled, he gets no liquid. When you take him out on a long outing, he should also be given water to drink.

2. *Food*

(i) *What?*

Your pup can be started right away on one of the proprietary balanced meals or canned puppy foods. Commercial foods are still looked upon with suspicion by some people, but they are manufactured under laboratory-tested conditions, and the dogs fed on proprietary balanced foods receive all the nutrients they require to grow and to develop resistance to disease. However, some commercial products, including some of the more expensive, consist entirely of meat products and do not contain all the necessary vitamins and minerals which must be supplied in other ways.

A dog needs proteins, fats, carbohydrates, vitamins and minerals to keep him in a healthy condition. These nutrients are obtained from a variety of sources, including meat and fishmeal, vegetable seeds and oils, milk proteins and cooked cereals. In some foods these are combined in the proportion to ensure that every single recommended nutrient known to be required by a dog is present at the correct level.

Puppies

Most breeders, when they sell their pups, give their new owners a diet sheet. This is often unnecessarily complicated and confuses the new owners. However, changing home will already have brought plenty of shocks and surprises for a young puppy so try to follow it, or at least give similar kinds of food at first. Then change the menu when the pup has settled in. Unless you are prepared to plan a diet carefully to ensure that your dog gets the right balance of nutrients you will probably find it better, and certainly more convenient, to go straight on to one of the ready formulated, canned, dry or semi-moist foods which already contain them in the correct proportions. Always make sure that there is clean, fresh water available. If you feed your dog dried foods then plenty of water is particularly needed

This growing period is vital in your dog's life. He must get the correct food, and enough food while his bones are forming. This is especially so with a large breed of dog.

Adult dogs

Fresh meat can be given either raw or cooked. Offal, which is cheaper than muscle meat, is usually rich in vitamins. But do not give liver to a dog which is suffering from diarrhoea or looseness, for it is laxative in effect. Household scraps which are fresh will often add welcome vitamins and minerals which are not present in muscle meat—but do not offer leftovers which have been left out and might have become contaminated. Your dog must never get only meat. He must get carbohydrates in his diet as well. Naturally you can mix fresh meat and canned foods, dried foods, biscuits and moist foods.

But with small breeds you must be careful not to make their diet too rich in protein, as this often causes skin problems.

If you can't afford to add meat to your dog's food, but your dog won't eat it plain, you can try out a few of these ideas.

You can prepare your dog's food with water which has been used to rinse out tasty household pots or empty meat-cans (freshly opened, or they may be contaminated). You can mix scraps of meat, gravy or vegetables from the table with his food (avoiding spicy and exotic cooking). If your dog is not overweight, you can pour a dessertspoonful of vegetable oil over his food. A little milk can also be poured over his food to encourage him to eat.

Your dog will also like, and benefit from, a drink of milk occasionally.

If your dog is hungry before he's due for his meal, you can give him some dog chews. They're good for his teeth to chew on, and he'll enjoy them. They provide no nourishment but keep him occupied.

If your dog has had an illness your vet may recommend a special diet for him. A dog, for instance, that has had liver trouble should be on a low protein diet and a dog that's lost a lot of blood from an injury should get raw liver (120-220 g daily for 14 days). Whenever a vet suggests a special diet after an illness, it should always be carefully adhered to.

(ii) *How often?*

Large dogs

2–7 months:	3 square meals a day
7–12 months:	2 square meals a day
Adult dogs: ·	1 square meal a day

This can vary. Very large dogs may need three meals a day until they're about nine months old, and two meals until they're about eighteen months old.

Small dogs

Under 2 months:	4 square meals a day
2–5 months:	3 square meals a day
5–7 months:	2 square meals a day
Adult dogs:	1 square meal a day

Don't stick rigidly to this table if your dog is overweight, or if he obviously needs more or less food. It has become fashionable to drop a pup's midday and morning meals too early, but a rickety, undernourished pup is as difficult to cure as one that's overfed. While a dog is still growing, one meal is not sufficient for him and people are all too often encouraged to underfeed their dogs, the hazards of overweight assuming exaggerated proportions and concealing the real dangers of under-feeding a hungry adolescent youngster growing at an astonishing rate.

(iii) *How much?*

Be guided by your dog's appetite (his individual meta-bolism), provided, of course, that he's not a guts, whether he's over or underweight, the amount of exer-cise he gets, his size, and the climate.

The amount of food required varies considerably between small breeds and big dogs—but that does not necessarily mean that, weight for weight, big dogs require more in the same proportion, although big-breed puppies may in the growing stage. Puppies need much more food than adults of comparable size, as a rough guide perhaps twice as much. For adults you can get some idea of the food requirement by allowing about 50 g per kilo body weight but there are so many factors to be taken into consideration that it is much better to keep a check on the dog's weight and make sure that you are neither over- nor under-feeding it.

Small dogs get as much as they want, unless they're overweight, in which case their food is *gradually* cut down. Tiny dogs usually have very small appetites and may even be disinclined to eat every day—usually to the consternation of their owners! On the other hand, they may like two smaller meals a day. They're inexpensive to feed, so one can afford to indulge their tastes a little. As long as they're frisky, wet-nosed and bright-eyed, they're getting enough food.

If your dog's ribs protrude or he's always looking at you with longing eyes in the kitchen, he's not getting enough food. If he's lean and muscular (this doesn't apply to immature dogs, and some breeds like *Labradors*, which are, by nature, well padded), nicely covered and glossy, you're feeding him correctly. But if he's like a barrel, walking with a rolling gait, he should have his food reduced and his exercise *gradually* increased.

(iv) *How and When?*

Give your dog freshly-prepared food in a wide-based bowl. Feed him in a quiet spot away from household traffic and away from a dominant companion. Feed him out of the sun or rain. (When you wash your dog's dishes, never wash them with those of the family—there is always the risk of infecting the family.)

A good time to feed a dog is early in the evening, so that he has a chance to relieve himself before he goes to sleep, and is clean at night. If you feed your dog before you have your dinner, the smell of cooking won't attract him to drool in the kitchen.

Your dog may gobble his food down at once, he may take his time over it, or he may voluntarily split it into meals. In the hot weather, the food he leaves should be refrigerated, and it can then be dished up to him the next day.

(v) *And what-not*

If a dog is fed sweets and cakes occasionally, I don't suppose his health will suffer any more than his owner's does (probably less, because he runs around a lot more). But he'll be more restful without wondering what goodies may be coming his way each time he hears the clink of tea-cups. Also, some dogs become fussy feeders if they're given a piece of bacon at breakfast, chocolate cake at tea, and then presented with balanced ration for supper.

However, dogs that get sweets, cakes and biscuits every day, and don't run around a lot to burn up the extra calories, get very fat, their hearts can't take the strain, they puff and pant with each step they have to climb and their teeth soon fall out—it's really not kind to them.

. . . puff and pant with each step

(vi) Supplements

Many dogs will get all the vitamin and mineral supplements they need in their regular proprietary foods but large dogs do sometimes become rickety if they do not get enough calcium. Calcium powders or tablets will help build up their bones while they're growing. They can be obtained from your pet shop. Directions for use are clearly stated on the label and, because too much can do as much harm as too little, should be followed carefully. Elderly dogs need an increase in both calcium and phosphorus and should not be subjected to abrupt changes in diet.

(vii) Bones

Bones are enjoyed by dogs and pups. A marrow bone keeps a dog happily occupied, provides him with minerals and nutrition, keeps his teeth clean, and helps a puppy with teething. People are sometimes advised not to give bones to their dogs because it's said that they make them constipated, or that they wear down the enamel on their teeth. But provided they are given in moderation, they won't cause constipation. And if dogs chew to such an extent that they wear down the enamel on their teeth — they should find a better way of passing such long hours!

No dog should be given chop bones, chicken bones, fish bones, or any other bones that splinter. They may puncture his intestines, or, in the case of chop bones, get stuck in his teeth. It's sometimes believed that the bones of battery chickens are young and soft enough for a dog to chew, but these can still perforate a dog's intestines.

(viii) *Old dogs*

As your dog gets older and gets less and less exercise, he'll tend to put on weight, unless his food intake is reduced. He may also like to have his meal split—half in the morning and half in the evening. He will also need more water when he gets older—preferably available to him 24 hours a day. This is essential for the proper functioning of an old dog's kidneys.

CHAPTER 4

DOG-BREEDING

Those who make the decision to breed from their bitch either do so because they want to make a bit of money or so that their children (or they themselves) can enjoy the experience of watching their bitch whelp and rear a litter; or because they feel it's good for their dog— physically, psychologically or both.

Is dog-breeding really profitable? If you have champion dogs and can demand a high price—perhaps. But the services of the stud are expensive, and when the bitch is mated she needs extra care and feeding supplement, especially while she's nursing her litter. The vet is usually required, and while suitable homes are being found the hungry litter devours four meals a day—then there's the cost of advertising when they're ready to go.

Taking all this into consideration, and the work and inconvenience of caring for the pups, breeding dogs can be costly and hard work.

There is prevalent a misconception regarding the effect that breeding has on both male dogs and bitches. When one thinks of the strain of carrying, whelping and nursing, one wonders why it's so often believed that a bitch should be bred just once—for the sake of her health.

Nature puts pups first, and the bitch's nutritional needs come second, her body being drained for their nutrition. And then there's always the risk involved when she gives birth. Her health certainly doesn't suffer if she's deprived of this experience!

However, some people breed from their bitch because they think it's *psychologically* necessary for her. But—what she never knows she doesn't miss. Wasn't it Medea who said in Euripides' Greek tragedy, '. . . but she who ne'er hath born a child nor known, is nearer to felicity'? A bitch that's had a litter, on the other hand, often becomes restless and broody at the sound of sucking, squealing or even at the sight of any small animal. If a bitch is spayed *before* her first season—before her maternal instinct even *starts* to develop—she cannot experience this frustration.

Moreover, without her reproductive organs, she won't suffer at any time from phantom pregnancies, cysts, inflammation of the uterus and other ailments that befall unspayed bitches.

We must also consider, before we breed our dogs: Are we possibly swelling the ranks of the dogs in animal sanctuaries that are without homes?

You are going to become very attached to your bitch's puppies, and you don't want any of them to find themselves unwanted after their new owners find they've outgrown their puppy charm, or decide they can't afford to feed them, or kennel them when they go on holiday; or get rid of them because they get too big, too boisterous or too troublesome; or because they've tired of boasting about the high price they paid for their dog, and showing off their swanky pedigree.

Season

Your bitch may have her first season any time from seven to twelve months old, then every six months or so. An upset or a disturbance (a visit to the kennels, for example) may bring this on earlier, or delay it, and sometimes a bitch that is very deeply attached to her owner may barely come into season, if at all. But this doesn't happen very often.

A bitch's season lasts for about three weeks and is recognized by a slight discharge and swelling of the external sex organ. She's only fertile roughly from about the tenth to the fourteenth day of her season (two days before she starts to ovulate and three days after she completes ovulating). The scent of her heat excites male dogs from the moment she comes into heat, and they can detect it from a long way off.

If you don't know when your bitch started her season, you can't count the days. But *she* knows when she's fertile. That's when she's set on finding a mate and, when she does, she flirts and pops her tail obligingly to one side for his convenience. She will usually stand like this for any dog—so eager is she that she doesn't distinguish male from female. When you pet her, she'll probably do it for you too! Although she attracts male dogs before she is fertile, she is not interested in them until she is fertile—and then she is as eager to find a mate as he is to reach her. Keep a very close watch on her at this time—she'll become very restless and anxious to get out.

She also advertises her presence and her condition by leaving little love letters around for her prospective suitors to read. They read, and get the message, and come quickly to make a date. Take her outside, and she'll drop these messages everywhere she goes in the form of a trickle of urine here, and there and everywhere, and there'll be a clamour at your front door.

There are both injections and pills available to postpone your dog's season. These are particularly useful if, for instance, a stud you are wanting to use isn't available at the moment, or you are going on holiday when your bitch is due to come into season, or if, for some other reason, you want to delay her season.

The pills and injections each have their own particular advantages and disadvantages, which you can discuss with your vet.

Sometimes when a bitch doesn't conceive, she may develop a phantom pregnancy. Even if she hasn't been mated, this can still happen. (The chapter on first aid deals with phantom pregnancies in detail.)

Family Planning

Dog-breeding takes place at three levels: casual mating amongst strays; planned or unplanned mongrel pet breeding, and the breeding of pedigreed dogs. There is a world-wide population explosion amongst dogs. Many of them are unwanted and in Britain many thousands are put down each year. Several hundred dogs *each day* are put to sleep in our country because they are not wanted. Most of them are strays and are not within the scope of this book, but too many of them began as pets—even expensive pedigreed pets.

Should you feel that there is a demand for your breed of dog—amongst people who you know will give the pups proper care—plan your family carefully.

Firstly, choose with care the time of year that you decide to breed your dog. If the pups are due to go to their new homes at holiday time, especially over Christmas, you won't have the same selection of homes to choose from. Christmas time is a bad time for placing pups. Not only are pups more likely to be bought on an impulse instead of after careful consideration, but people are away, and are preoccupied with Christmas festivities. And pups that are given away as presents are not always wanted by those who receive them.

Secondly, before you breed from your bitch, has she a sound temperament, being neither nervous nor vicious? Is she healthy, with no hereditary ailments? (See under choosing a healthy dog.) Is she old enough to breed? If she is still immature, breeding from her will impair her development. Is she young enough? It is not always easy for a dog to have her first litter after she's four years old. A dog that is bred regularly can have pups without undue risk until she is about six or seven years old. After this, complications are, naturally, more likely to arise as she gets older, and there is more risk to her life as she begins to age and her muscles become weaker. And if you have bred from her before, she shouldn't be bred from more than once a year.

Is she registered with the Kennel Club? Because if she's not, *her* pups can't be registered.

When you choose a father for your pups, is *he* registered, is he good-natured, and free from any hereditary ailments?

Sometimes when the subject of hereditary ailments is raised with breeders before using their stud, they hedge and get stuffy. Go elsewhere. The *Kennel Gazette* carries advertisements of dogs at stud and the various breed clubs will supply stud lists for their particular breed.

The father of your pups is important, because half of his genes will be going to your pups. Get to know him, see how good he is with children, and how stable his temperament is.

You may, on occasions, be advised to check their pedigrees to see that they have ancestors in common — and on other occasions, that they haven't.

Inbreeding

There is so much controversy regarding inbreeding (interbreeding). Man defies his own taboo and inbreeds his pedigreed dogs.

All living creatures carry genes that determine how they look and behave. Hereditary factors such as hair colour, height, temperament, beauty, and so on, are all transmitted via these genes. Some of these hereditary factors are apparent, and some aren't. The apparent factors are transmitted via single or double *dominant* genes, or double *recessive* genes, and the unseen factors are transmitted via single recessive genes. This is how brown-eyed parents can have a blue-eyed child—provided both brown-eyed parents carry a recessive gene for blue eyes.

When two parents are closely related, they are more likely to be carrying the *same* recessive genes, which will therefore get more chance to pair up in some of their offspring, thereby becoming apparent. These characteristics are not apparent in the parents, but they become apparent in the offspring, because the genes doubled up—one from each parent.

But if parents are in no way related to one another, they carry many different and varied genes—both dominant and recessive. The recessive genes *may* be transmitted, but do *not* become apparent unless each parent transmits the same recessive gene to any of their offspring. Because the recessive genes carried by these unrelated parents are so varied, they don't get the chance to double up that often and their offspring do not, therefore, manifest these unseen hereditary factors.

Inbreeding is condemned because any *harmful* recessive genes that may be present get much more opportunity to double up. This is not to say, however, that two related dogs do both carry any similar harmful recessive genes, or, on the other hand, that two unrelated dogs do not have the same harmful genes.

Most harmful genes are recessive, and at present it is quite impossible to say which animal is carrying what unseen hereditary factor without lengthy and carefully controlled breeding experiments.

Breeders usually mate grandsire to granddaughter to make it *less* likely that similar harmful recessive genes will pair up in their litters, than if they mated father to daughter and brother to sister, for instance—although this is practised fairly frequently.

These breeders are trying to emphasize certain points in their dogs, such as tail carriage, and so on, that will bring them show points, but so often, together with these sought-after external conformations go hereditary ailments, such as hip dysplasia and blindness, for instance.

Consistent inbreeding leads to a general lack of vigour in both plants and animals, a deterioration in bone structure, and a low resistance, both mentally and physically.

Dog-breeders refuse to acknowledge this fact because by consistently inbreeding their dogs they achieve the 'correct' physical conformations, like length of body in *Dachshunds*, narrow heads in *Collies*, broad heads in *Bulldogs*, coat texture in *Poodles*—and not too many spots in *Dalmatians*. To achieve these ends, and thereby make their dogs show champions, and thus put up the price of their puppies and stud fees, they achieve financial gain.

So these breeders go all out to make their dogs, not as nature meant them to be, but as someone, some-where, sometime ago, decided they should be. *Bulldogs* can't give birth, *Dachshunds* need six legs, *Yorkshire Terriers* go around in curlers, and the bone structure of some dogs is so flimsy that they are crippled with arthritis, from ailments such as hip dysplasia, and their nerves so jittery, that they jump in terror every time a door creaks.

No one has yet said 'hip dysplasia is a direct result of in-breeding' so loudly that any heed is taken, but if inbred sheep, for instance, die in a cold spell and mongrel sheep can stand up to the rigours of extreme climate, it stands to reason that other animals will suffer similar adverse affects from inbreeding.

This is not, however, to condemn the breeding of pedigreed dogs altogether. To breed a dog of good quality, which is not inbred, the correct procedure is to line-breed.

The dogs in the same blood-line are not too closely related, but are of the same family. And if another similar blood-line is introduced from time to time to prevent the dogs from becoming inbred, this procedure is highly desirable—and is carried out by the reputable breeders who have a regard for the welfare of the dogs they breed in their kennels.

Without line-breeding, breeding is haphazard, but when carried too far, it produces the sad results we've just discussed.

Mating

If you haven't dewormed your bitch recently, do this, because if she has any roundworms these may be transferred to the developing embryos. Three weeks after mating, however, no bitch should be dewormed.

Don't allow the mating to take place without being present yourself. A pedigree certificate states that the father on the pedigree certificate is actually the father of the pups—and if you weren't there, how can you certify it?

Moreover, your bitch may be uneasy if you leave her, and may not co-operate during the mating. Others, however, may behave in the opposite way and refuse to co-operate if you are there. This is why breeders are sometimes wary of owners of bitches interfering and fussing, and causing upset and delay during the mating. Set aside a whole day. Let the dogs get to know each other. Don't rush them, and let the experts supervise the union.

If you have an experienced breeder, leave it to him, and don't upset your bitch by interfering. Keep calm and do not excite the dogs.

The dogs should have an area spacious enough for them to play and flirt in, but where they can still be controlled and receive no interference from other dogs.

Introduce them on leads, should they take an instant dislike to one another. When they are acquainted, leave them, but keep an eye on them all the same—the stud may, for instance, have difficulty in mounting, or your bitch may try to bite him, or injure him during the mating.

If the stud fails in his first attempt to mate, he should be taken away to cool off, given a drink of water, and reintroduced when he's quietened down.

When they mate, they will lock. The male dog will turn, and they will stand back to back for about 20 minutes to half an hour. This is when they should be watched, because they can be injured if your bitch tries to lie down or escape. If your bitch sags under his weight, she should be gently supported until the stud turns. However, if no tie is achieved, it is not unusual for the bitch to still conceive. Most breeders provide two matings for the stud fee.

The Use of a Stud

A stud can be used from the time he's mature—and can be mated on alternate days. If he's used on two consecutive days, however, he must have a break of two days. If he's used twice on one day, a rest of three days is needed to build up his fertility again. A stud should be fed a well-balanced diet and be given a lot of exercise to keep him in peak condition.

Pregnancy

Once your bitch is mated, she should get regular exercise all through her pregnancy—but, of course, no wild play or strain.

How do you know whether your bitch has conceived? This is where your patience is put to the test! Your vet can't tell until about 28 to 35 days after the mating, depending on her breed and her figure. Then he should be able to feel the developing embryo—but be patient, and you'll see her take on a matronly appearance within a short while, should all have gone well.

A teaspoonful of cod liver oil every day will be good for her, and, after the first two or three weeks, give her two meals a day. As her pregnancy advances, give her as much to eat as she wants—she needs it with anything up to eleven or more new pups developing inside her! A bitch should get her food increased by 50%, with plenty of milk providing the vital calcium, and extra protein—liver, cheese and eggs being excellent supplements.

Whelping

Give your bitch a comfortable bed to whelp in, big enough for her to stretch out in comfortably. Place it in a warm and private part of the house, where the pups will have space to run around when they start growing, and where it will be easy for you to keep clean. Some big dogs may lie on a pup and kill or injure it. A specially made box with a rail around, as illustrated, will prevent this. Introduce your bitch to her bed well in advance of her whelping so that she is used to it and will be happy to whelp in it.

Don't arrange to go out too much when the pups are due. This will be about 63 days after the mating. Tell your vet what date the pups are due, should you need him. Some breeds, such as *Bulldogs* and *Pugs*, have difficulty in whelping. Consult your vet and experts on the breed for guidance on how to cope. Their heads are usually too large (the pups') for their mother's pelvis, and a Caesarean section is often necessary.

When your bitch is due to whelp, her temperature will drop slightly, there will be a slight discharge and she will get restless, trying to make a nest to whelp in.

When she starts to give birth she'll want you near — but not all the friends and neighbours, because this will upset her. If it's a hot day, give her a cool spot, and if it's cold, a warm room. If you are advised to pull and poke while she's labouring—don't! A layman can easily injure a pup while trying to help.

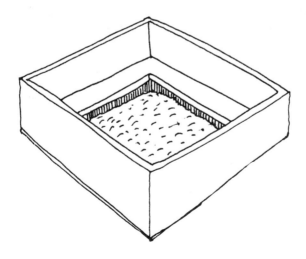

If your bitch is straining and in difficulty, her distress will be obvious, and you must summon your vet immediately. If she strains for more than $2\frac{1}{2}$ hours, the vet's assistance is definitely needed. But she will more than likely cope admirably. It is also better if you don't walk her around between the birth of each pup.

Just remain calm; offer her water or milk; reassure her; and let her have peace and quiet, calling the vet if necessary.

There should be an interval of about fifteen minutes to half an hour (depending on her size) between each pup, during which time she will rest or lick and nurse those that have been born. As soon as the pups are born, she will free them from their embryonic sac and bite the umbilical cord free. Then she will eat the afterbirth.

Always see to it that she has ample liquid at hand during her whelping.

While the pups are being born, leave them with your bitch. She will get distressed if they're removed and the pups will have a better chance to drink her cholostrum, which she only produces on the first day or so. This cholostrum gives the pups the vital antibodies they must have to build up their resistance to disease for the first couple of months of their lives. (Should your pups for some reason receive no cholostrum, they must be inoculated when they're two weeks old.) Also, if the pups are removed as soon as they're born, there is always the possibility that she may disregard them when they are returned.

If you are doubting whether they have all been born, a retained pup will cause her pain, and she will not have the contented maternal expression that comes after the birth of all the pups. She will run a temperature, and there will be a foul-smelling discharge as the retained pup begins to decompose. Unless she is treated immediately, she will die.

When the birth is over, take your bitch out for a run, change the bedding, give her warm milk with glucose, and leave her to sleep.

If her stools are rather black and large for a couple of days after the birth of her pups, don't be concerned, this is quite normal. Your bitch will bleed for about two weeks after the birth of her pups.

Nursing

If your bitch has long hair, clip the hair around her teats to give the pups easy access to their milk supply. If her nipples get hard and cause her pain when the pups suckle, rub them gently with a little olive oil. If suckling is still painful, she may have a condition known as mastitis. (See later.)

When the pups are one to three days old, their dew claws should be removed, and if she is of a breed that has its tails docked, that should be done at the same

To dock or not to dock?

time. Most dogs benefit from having their dew claws removed, because they serve no purpose, and may become ingrown or injured. The vet should do this for you. A layman may cause injury to the pup if he is inexperienced and tries to do it himself.

Whether or not you have your pups' tails docked depends on their breed—*Poodles*, *Boxers* and *Spaniels*, for example, have their tails docked. Although the operation has recently been proclaimed unethical, it is still practised.

If it is done properly, the pup feels very little pain, but if his tail hasn't been docked at this early age, it cannot be done when he's older.

All things considered, it's a practice that dates from barbarous times. It distinguished working dogs, which were non-taxable, from pets, which were taxable and— people being people—all sorts of breeds got docked! And with some breeds, the practice has persisted until modern times.

But the absence of an excited tail in the house does undoubtedly save the odd cup and saucer from going for a burton! And there's a lot to be said for that!

Now that the pups have been born, give your bitch plenty of food. It all goes into her milk so she will get hungry. Give her three meals a day, and ample milk.

Provide extra warmth only if necessary. A heater in the room will provide an even temperature when it's cold. Otherwise, let her room be well ventilated—but draught-free, and just comfortably warm.

Don't distress your dog by allowing too many strangers in, or by taking the pups out of her sight, or handling them too much.

When the pups get bigger, let them get used to being

handled gently, so that they're completely confident, and are quite used to people when they go to their new homes.

Your bitch knows what's best for her pups. Let her come and go to them as she feels she wants to. The more exercise she gets the better (but don't force her against her will). As they get older, she will leave them for longer periods, especially when their teeth and nails get sharp. She must never be forced to stay with her pups.

If she wants to bite anyone who touches or comes near her pups, don't discourage it, or be alarmed—it's perfectly normal for a brood bitch to protect her pups in this way.

The pups' umbilical cords will fall off after two or three days; their eyes will open in twelve to fifteen days; their ears will open in fifteen to seventeen days and they'll start blinking when they're about sixteen days old. They will achieve visual orientation at twenty-one days and sound orientation when they are twenty-five days old.

When your pups are between nine and twelve days old, they'll double their birth weight! (Thanks to the 'old girl' who supplies the means for them to do it!)

For the first ten days, the pups will need the warmth of their mother and each other for their survival (or, if they're orphaned, artificial heat—see later).

Start advertising your litter early. If you leave it too late, your pups start losing their puppy appeal as they get older—and cost you more each day as their appetites grow.

If your bitch is registered with the Kennel Club,

make application to register her litter when they are about a week old. (See page 53)

Start writing out your pedigrees early. Otherwise you have quite a chore waiting for you when they're ready to go! The new owners will be wanting to take the pedigree certificates together with the pups.

For the first three weeks or so, it's easy to care for the pups. Mum does all the work. She feeds and cleans them, and they just sleep all day. The best you can do for them is to see that they all get a fair share, and that no pup is allowed to be pushed aside all the time. After that, however, comes the hard work—they must be weaned and they must be allowed to run around and play about in a suitable area which must be kept clean. It must have shade, but mustn't be too cold for them.

Sometimes a bitch may develop mastitis. Her teats will become congested and painful and discharge a brownish, infected, fluid, which will cause the pups to die if the condition is not cured. This can happen any time within the first thirty days after whelping. It is obvious when a bitch is suffering from mastitis because of her reluctance to go to her pups and her distress. She should be taken to the vet immediately.

A shortage of calcium can also cause complications. The dog stiffens, and may even take fits. The vet can relieve this condition immediately with calcium injections, but, to prevent it, give your bitch plenty of milk to drink.

Weaning the Pups

Start weaning your pups when they're three weeks old. Give them some scraped meat, or a little mince, or

132

some tinned dogs' meat, or something that's equally tasty. Put a little on their noses—they'll lick it off, and soon get the idea! Give them a taste first, then a tea-spoonful, gradually increasing the amount, as their appetites demand. Then put them on to a little mince and baby cereal, starting with once or twice a day, and increasing it to three times a day. When they are five weeks old, feed them three times a day on the diet suggested on page 109. Your bitch will also regurgitate her own food to help wean them. This is good for the pups—but, remember, Mum will be hungry again!

This early weaning is important, because without it the demands the pups make on your bitch are too great a strain on her.

Before letting them go, it is important that you deworm them for roundworm. Follow the directions carefully (see page 144) and advise their new owners how to continue with the deworming programme.

Should you have a pup in your litter that's really a little runt, nervous and unhappy, rather than give him to people where he'll bring a lot of anxiety, and be an unhappy little animal—have him put down.

Placing the Pups

Provided they're weaned, the pups of most breeds are ready to go to their new homes when they're about seven weeks old. If you wait until they are older before placing them, the poor mother has to endure sharp teeth and scratching claws for those extra weeks. The pups are also draining her of nutrition when she should be recovering from the strain of whelping and nursing. If she's relieved of them when they're seven weeks old, she'll be only too pleased to see the back of the little blighters—and the new owners will also enjoy having their new pup that much sooner.

Choose their homes carefully. Chapter 18 will give you hints on how you select the best homes for them. Don't let all the pups go at once—it will be very distressing for your bitch. If they go over a period of a few days, she'll accept it quite easily. Advise the new owners carefully how to feed and care for their new pup.

If you decide to keep one of your bitch's puppies and find that he doesn't form a proper attachment to you, this is probably because he hasn't been separated from his mother; sometimes a dog doesn't develop his own complete personality until he's 'broken the apron strings'.

Orphaned Pups

Should you have the misfortune of having orphaned pups, or should your bitch for some reason reject her offspring, you will have the very hard work of rearing them by hand.

Firstly, they'll need warmth. This may be suppiied by a heater near your pups' bedding. The room must be well ventilated but without draught. During the first week, a thermometer in your pups' bed should read between 30 and 31°C (90 and 92°F). A virus which causes fading puppy disease (where the pups just get weak and die) thrives at lower temperatures.

Feed your pups with a doll's bottle. A dropper is too quickly emptied. Don't squeeze the bottle—let the pup suck the milk out. A bitch's milk is much richer than cow's milk, and, in an emergency, a formula of half a cup of cow's milk to one teaspoonful of sweetened condensed milk at 38°C (101°F) will resemble a bitch's milk. The milk must always be fresh and not stored warm, but refrigerated. The formula should be made up fresh each day. More convenient, and specially formulated for rearing puppies and kittens, is Lactol, a vitamin-fortified milk powder which is mixed with water. A feeding table according to age and type is given on the tin. You should be able to get it from your chemist or pet supplier.

The most common mistake when preparing a feed for orphan puppies is to take a look at the tiny wee pup, and compare it with a day-old calf, and come to the understandable conclusion that surely the cow's milk will have to be very diluted before the pup can drink it! In fact, the very reverse is the case. Cow's milk has a cream content of roughly 4%, mother's milk, 3%, bitch's milk as much as 11%, and goat's milk 7%.

Another suitable feed for an orphan pup is the skim of jersey milk (if you live in an area where it is obtainable) after it has been standing a while for the cream to accumulate.

Always give your orphan pup his food perfectly fresh, and roughly at body temperature.

Feed the pups when they awaken. If they suck in air, bring up the wind after each feed by rubbing their tummy very gently. They may or may not break a wind, depending on how greedily they drink their feed.

The mother bitch licks her pup's bottoms after each meal, and this way they relieve themselves. Unless you do this for them, they won't survive. However, a piece of cotton wool dipped in warm water and squeezed out will do the trick. Rub this gently over the pup's excretory organs until they oblige. Then dry the area well. The pups may get 'nappy rash'. To avoid this, put a little Nivea on after each session.

Orphaned pups

If a pup gets diarrhoea, put half a teaspoonful of cornflour in his feed until his tummy has righted itself. If a pup gets constipated, put two drops of liquid paraffin in his bottle. If you are in any doubt, consult your vet.

If the pups received no cholostrum from their mother, they must be inoculated when they are 2 weeks old.

Follow the weaning programme, as described above, when the pups are three weeks old.

To Spay or Not to Spay

Ask your vet's advice about the best time to spay your bitch. Some vets may advise you to let your bitch have a litter first, but it really doesn't benefit her in any way, and causes you a lot of inconvenience. It is often said that having a litter quietens a dog—but it's said equally as often that spaying her does!

Some dogs, once they're spayed, put on weight, but this is not usually the case. If a bitch puts on weight after she's spayed, she should be given more exercise, and her diet regulated.

Because kennelling is expensive, a mongrel litter not always easy to place, and a scheming bitch confined indoors is inconvenient—spay her!

One may argue that spaying is unnatural, but nature made dogs to breed so profusely to allow for the many natural enemies which do not, of course, prey on their litters any longer—so that argument doesn't hold!

The spaying fee is high, but the vet, on his own, has the total responsibility for the dog's life. He has to do the anaesthetizing, he has to sterilize and he has to operate —in other words he's surgeon, anaesthetist, theatre sister and stooge all in one. The wound has to be a small and careful incision because the dog will be walking that same day, not lying on her back for a week! Taking all this into consideration—and the knowledge that you will now have a dog without breeding problems and without divided loyalties—it's well worth it!

Should your bitch come into season sooner than you expect, and you don't want to be bothered with kennelling and so on, the operation is bigger and a little more expensive—but most vets will still undertake to do it.

A bitch confined indoors can be inconvenient

Sometimes when a bitch has been spayed, she may start attracting male dogs again. The bitch probably has an infection, or perhaps a foreign body, like a grass seed, lodged in her vagina. The vet will diagnose the condition and treat her for you.

Accidental Mating

If your bitch is accidentally mated, the vet can give her an injection to terminate her pregnancy—provided she's taken to him within forty-eight hours of mating.

However, should your dog be pedigreed, and she was 'caught by a travelling man', she can still produce puppies as pedigreed as ever after the misalliance on subsequent pregnancies, whether the pregnancy is terminated or allowed to continue.

Male Dogs

And male dogs? Male dogs are also better off without their misguided owners seeking to fulfil their sex lives (their dogs', that is). Once they've been mated, naturally enough they seek to repeat this experience, possibly becoming chronic wanderers. If a dog never comes into contact with a bitch in season, he really doesn't know what he's missing! And he's better off without it.

Castration is dealt with under canine casanovas in the chapter on problem dogs.

Cryptorchidism

Some dogs have only one testicle that descends into the scrotum. This is an hereditary condition, and breeding from monorchid dogs is discouraged.

The retained testicle may have to be removed if it causes problems.

CHAPTER 5

HEALTH AND FIRST AID

Your Vet

If you are in an area where you have a choice of vet, choose with care. Choose a vet who is gentle with animals in pain, and who is prepared to see your pet outside surgery hours in the case of an emergency. You will find a list of vets in the Yellow Pages under Veterinary Surgeons and Practitioners.

Your vet is going to be your dog's best friend for the rest of his life. When you take your pup for his inoculations, this is the time he will meet you and your pup, and you will get to know each other.

Always be considerate towards your vet—only consult him during his surgery hours, and remember that he is a busy man with heavy responsibilities. Follow his instructions carefully, and don't phone or worry him unless it is absolutely necessary.

When you take your dog to your vet, you can save him time, and make his diagnosis easier for him by noting your dog's symptoms carefully: the nature and regularity of his motions (or vomiting); his appetite; whether he's drinking water excessively; if he's lethargic, and so on.

When your dog is ill, and the vet makes a diagnosis, I would suggest that you ask him to explain the illness, and the treatment he is giving your dog.

Accidents happen, so have not only your vet's number handy but also that of the local animal hospital, which, by its very name, has someone on standby at all hours.

Should you not be satisfied with the progress your dog is making under treatment, the ethical approach is to ask your vet to refer you to another, so that they can consult together on your dog's condition.

In the event of an accident or an emergency, take your dog to your vet. If you call him to the scene of the accident, he may not have all the equipment he may need with him. However, should an injured dog try to bite anyone who comes near and no one can handle him, the vet may have to be called to sedate him—but all this wastes valuable time when his life may be in danger. (Another circumstance which would warrant calling a vet out would be in the event of strychnine poisoning, when moving the dog can cause his death, or after a convulsion, when your dog shouldn't be disturbed any further. See later.)

Inoculations

When your pup is three months old, you must take him to your vet for his inoculations. Until this age, he has an immunity which he acquired from the antibodies in his mother's cholostrum—the liquid which she produces during the first day or two after whelping and before her milk appears.

He has now lost this immunity and is in danger of getting distemper, and hardpad—illnesses which are fatal to dogs. He should then have a booster one year later, when he is about fifteen months old. This should give him immunity for the rest of his life.

However, if your dog leads a sheltered life and doesn't mix with other dogs, he'll lose this immunity, and should receive further boosters.

Some illnesses are prevalent only in certain areas, and your vet will advise you as to whether your dog will need any further inoculations.

Medical Aid

While your pup is still tiny, it is well worth considering taking out a pet's medical insurance policy. You'll be glad of it if you are landed with any unexpected large vet bills. This may not cover minor ailments, but insures you against any ailment or accident which is going to entail too heavy a vet's bill.

Don't wait for the contingency to arise—then it's too late. Should your dog at any stage need major treatment, your vet will want to be able to give him the best treatment possible—so, when you attend to your pup's inoculations, consult your insurance agent on your dog's medical aid policy as well—and you're covered.

At the same time you would be wise to take out a policy to cover you for any liability should your dog inadvertently inflict any damage or cause an accident.

If you want to take out these policies, do it when you

get your dog, not when you lose him or get your vet bill or the postman gets bitten—then it's too late!

Parasites

All dogs should be kept free of parasites. Parasites can be a public health hazard and a health hazard to the family.

However, we don't just refuse to own a motor car because people have accidents in them, but we take precautions to drive carefully. Similarly we don't refuse to keep a dog because of the parasites he may harbour, but we keep him free of fleas and worms.

This, fortunately, is easy and inexpensive.

We ourselves do not get worms from dogs, but we may act as the intermediary host in the life-cycle of some of the worms a dog may harbour.

It is not very common for a person to pick up an egg and become a host, but it has been known to happen, and because it is so cheap and easy to keep a dog free of worms, we should take precautions against it.

The flea also acts as an intermediary host in the life-cycle of the tapeworm. (An intermediary host does not itself have an intestinal infestation, but harbours the parasite at a stage between the egg and the worm—something like a caterpillar between an egg and a moth. Although hardly strictly accurate, the comparison provides a rough parallel.)

To keep your dog free of worms, deworm him every six months. Worm pills, if administered as directed, are completely harmless to your dog, and can have no harmful side effects.

As an extra health precaution, never wash your dog's dishes with those of the family.

(a) Worms

One or more of the following symptoms will be present

in a dog that's infested with worms: his coat will probably be harsh and coarse to the touch; his breath offensive; his gums pale; he may cough; have an indifferent appetite, or eat ravenously; he may be listless, and lose weight. A dog that has tapeworm usually has little white segments like rice present in some of his stools (if this irritates him, he may rub his bottom on the ground), and if the infestation is bad, his sides will 'cave in'.

If a dog has tapeworm, his sides are hollow, and if he has roundworm, he is bloated. Dogs that are badly infested with roundworm have pot-bellies and yet their ribs protrude. They may also have long white worms in their stools or vomit them up.

However, a dog that looks healthy, and has a glossy coat may still have worms. *Regular* deworming is essential to both dog *and* family.

In different areas, dogs are prone to different internal parasites. When you take your pup for his inoculations, your vet can tell you what parasites are likely to infect your dog in your area, and you can consult him on detecting them and the best method of eradicating them.

There are various patent medicines available for worms, some being more effective than others. Patent medicines may not always be as effective as those you can obtain through your vet by prescription. You can't go very wrong with roundworm pills but consult the vet for tapeworm treatment which requires more careful prescribing.

When you deworm your dog, *follow the instructions carefully*. In order to administer the correct dosage, you must weigh your dog. I doubt if he'll oblige you by standing nicely on the scale, so weigh yourself first. Then weigh yourself with your dog in your arms and subtract the first weight from the second and you have your dog's weight.

And if you've got a *Great Dane*, you've got troubles!

Actually, it's easier than that. Dogs as large as Great Danes receive the maximum dosage. To administer the pills, conceal them in your dog's food, and put those he rejects into some mince or butter.

If you're deworming a small pup, break the tablet into half, or into quarters. Push one section of the pill into the back of his throat. Hold his head up and stroke his throat, or pour a teaspoonful of water into his mouth to make him swallow it. Repeat with each section until he's taken the correct dosage.

If you're deworming more than one dog, keep them apart—or you won't know who's had how many!

With a bad infestation, deworming a dog can cause his stools to be loose. It's best, then, to deworm him in the morning on a sunny day, when he can go outside afterwards.

You may have to repeat the dosage. Do this exactly as instructed on the package. This is because some of the preparations do not remove the eggs as well—and after a couple of weeks you're back to square one.

Two types of worms are present in all areas—roundworm and tapeworm.

The pills that remove tapeworm don't remove roundworm—and vice versa. The preparations for both can, however, be given simultaneously.

Tapeworms pass into a dog's body by way of an intermediary host—usually the flea. The fleas carry the eggs, the dog bites and ingests a flea, and is then infected.

Pups under three months don't usually pick up tapeworm, and it is not, as a rule, necessary to deworm a pup of this age for tapeworm. However, should you have reason to suspect a young pup of having tapeworm, take it (and a sample stool) to your vet, who will prescribe an appropriate simple treatment.

When you buy your pup, ask if he's been dewormed for roundworm. All pups should be dewormed for roundworms before they go to their new homes. If yours hasn't, do it as soon as you get him. Roundworm is widely prevalent, and passes from a bitch to her pups through her milk supply. Roundworms make pups anaemic and undernourished. Once they've been dewormed, however, their condition will pick up immediately.

(b) Fleas

Fleas can be controlled by dip, flea powder, aerosol spray, collars or shampoo. Powdering is easy, the effect lasts longer than dip, and it is inexpensive. Be careful not to inhale the powder or spray while applying it, as it is poisonous.

A bad infestation is best controlled by (1) administering a course of pills, obtainable from your vet, to all animals in the house (1 tablet per 20 lb twice a week). A course of treatment does the dog no harm and eradicates the fleas effectively in a few weeks, but they should not be given continuously. Always keep the pills out of the reach of children. (2) By giving the dog and his bedding a powdering each evening. The bedding must also be done because that is where the fleas breed.

Dog dip is easy to apply

(3) The fleas also breed in carpets, and once they've taken over (which can happen in the most respectable of households) fumigation is the only course. (4) Flea collars are widely used, but not recommended where small children handle the dog a lot.

(c) Ticks

Many people reluctantly deny their dogs a much-needed romp in the open for fear of ticks. Pills are available from vets which will ensure that any tick which bites that dog will die. Do not pull ticks straight off your dog—they may come apart, leaving the mouth parts behind, where they may cause a sore. Dab them with a little alcohol—any spirit will do—and they will let go. If ticks become established in the house they must be treated with a specifically tickoidal spray—not all insecticides affect the tick.

Symptoms of Ill-health

An elementary knowledge of the symptoms of illness and first aid measures may well save a dog's life. However, this is only intended as a general outline of the common ailments that may befall the household pet. More detailed diagnoses and treatment are, of course, the field of the qualified veterinary surgeon.

If your dog has badly-discharging eyes, a hot, dry nose, a temperature of over 39°C, pale gums, a swelling on any part of his body, repeated attacks of diarrhoea and/or vomiting; or if he refuses to eat, drinks excessive amounts of water, is preoccupied with licking or biting any part of his body, is unduly lethargic, restless or whining, rubs his ear on the ground or carries his head to one side, or displays any other symptoms suggesting he is in pain, or isn't well, he needs medical attention.

148

If your dog eats grass, don't worry. All dogs do this, and nature's sure to have a reason for it.

Medicines

When your vet prescribes medicine for your dog, ask him to explain the treatment your dog is getting. In some cases—particularly with antibiotics, the course must be completed, or else, as with people, the dog will develop a resistance to the antibiotic, and will not respond to treatment on future occasions. If, however, it is a pain-killer your dog is getting, he should not have any more than necessary.

Dogs have a higher resistance to pain than most people realize, and unless your vet advises you to give your dog painkillers, they are not usually necessary. In fact, painkillers may mask a dog's symptoms, and prevent a vet from making a correct diagnosis.

Unless the vet says to the contrary, all medicines that are not used up should be discarded.

Follow your vet's instructions carefully.

(a) Pills

If your dog doesn't swallow his pill greedily, he may if it's tucked away in his food or disguised in butter or mince. But if he's too ill to be tempted, push the pill right back into his throat and hold his head up and stroke his throat until he swallows. (A little milk or water poured into his throat will also make him swallow it.) If he struggles, be very firm with him. Place him between your knees and hold him firmly. If he's too strong, enlist the help of another person. If you're giving pills to a pup, break them into halves or quarters.

(b) Liquids

A little minced-beef-à-la-antibiotic is probably the best idea in administering medicine to a dog: if your dog's not too ill and is eating well, mix the medicine with a small quantity of his favourite food. But if he's too ill to eat, he's probably too ill to struggle anyway. So put small amounts of the liquid on to a spoon (so that, *should* he struggle, you won't lose it all), hold his head up, pull out the pouch of his lower lip at the corner of his mouth, and pour it in, and it'll slide down his throat. If he struggles, ask someone else to hold him for you, be firm and speak soothingly to him while you administer it.

Some medicines, however, a dog will lap up on his own—liquid paraffin, for instance, is considered a delicacy by most dogs.

Taking a Dog's Temperature

If you're in doubt as to whether your dog is ill or not, take his temperature. The normal temperature for a dog is about 38,6°C (101,5°F). A temperature over 39°C indicates a dog is ill, and he should receive medical attention. Use a heavy duty thermometer, for a dog's temperature is taken rectally.

To take his temperature, put vaseline on the thermometer, insert it gently into your dog's rectum, support him so that he cannot sit on it, and talk soothingly to him. Remove it after thirty seconds.

Some dogs struggle violently when having their temperature taken. If a dog in my kennels struggles when I take his temperature, I put him on a check chain, win his confidence, get him to lie down and stroke his tummy to make him relax. Having placed the greased thermometer near by, I put my knee on the check chain, close to his neck, continue to stroke him gently with my one hand and insert the thermometer gently with the other, soothing him all the while. If you cannot manage, however, rather take him to the vet.

Discharging Eyes

If your dog's eye is discharging because he has a slight infection, a little eye ointment from your vet will clear it up immediately, but don't use old ointment, throw it away, it may have picked up more germs than you are trying to kill. If both your dog's eyes are discharging, he has a temperature, he won't eat or is obviously unwell, he should be taken to the vet immediately, for the symptoms could indicate a more serious condition.

While you apply the eye ointment, soothe your dog, and hold the tube *parallel* to his eye so that you won't poke his eye if he jerks his head.

Apply the ointment frequently—three to four times a day—and if the infection doesn't clear immediately, he must be taken to the vet.

Remember, however, that a slight moist discharge in the corner of a dog's eye is normal. If your dog is bright-eyed, and obviously well you need not be concerned.

Earache

If your dog shakes his head—not the good hearty shake that you see in a dog that's brimming with vitality, but a slow careful shake, that indicates he is in pain—or carries his head on one side, rubs it on the ground, or scratches at it repeatedly, he has earache and is needing medical attention.

There are various causes of earache in a dog. The most frequent cause is an accumulation of wax which causes the ear canal to become inflamed—particularly when a dog's ears are pendulous or hairy, and the air cannot circulate in the ear canal. (See under the section on grooming for advice on the care of a dog's ears.)

A dog with earache may also have an infection in his ear or a foreign body, like a tick or a grass seed lodged in his ear, which only the vet can remove. There may also be a fungus growing in his ear canal.

Whatever is causing the irritation, the dog should be taken to the vet right away. The longer you leave it, the more difficult it will be for the vet to cure it.

Follow your vet's instructions carefully. When you apply the eardrops, massage the base of your dog's ear so that the drops penetrate right down into his ear canal.

Loss of Appetite

If your dog usually has a healthy appetite and suddenly goes off his food, he should be taken to the vet immediately. Sudden loss of appetite is an early symptom of some very serious illnesses. The more advanced the illness becomes, the more difficult it is to cure.

If your dog is perfectly healthy, and still refuses to eat, refer to page 299.

Dry Nose

A number of people have implicit faith in the diagnosis of all doggy illnesses by the detection of a damp nose. The dog may simply be thirsty! Yet he may also be very ill, while his nose is moist. A warm nose *may* indicate a temperature—but a thermometer is a sure way of telling you whether or not your dog is ill.

Diarrhoea

If your dog has diarrhoea, he may just have an upset stomach, or it may be a symptom of something more serious.

If he has a temperature, is vomiting, or isn't eating, he should be taken to the vet.

But if he's just suffering from a minor digestive upset—rather than dose him with anything, let it clear up on its own. A dog can usually rid its system of a slight food poisoning, and home remedies often cause further irritation. However, if your dog's stomach doesn't clear up after two or three days, he should see the vet.

Vomiting

Dogs, after they've swallowed something and then changed their minds about it, can usually voluntarily return it from their stomach. But if a dog that is vomiting looks miserable, has a temperature, brings up bile, has diarrhoea or pale gums, or refuses to eat, he obviously needs medical attention.

Hiccups

A small pup often gets hiccups when he eats too fast. This needn't cause any alarm—it's quite natural and he'll grow out of it.

Constipation

If your dog is constipated, give him more exercise. You can give him milk of magnesia, or a tablespoonful of liquid paraffin (which is easy to administer because dogs usually lap it up eagerly), but it shouldn't be given too often, as it absorbs the vitamins from the body. Wholewheat bread and liver will also help restore his stomach to normal. A dog that's constipated may also be needing a more balanced diet.

Swallowed Objects

Lively young pups have a habit of trying to taste the most unusual assortment of objects. They can sometimes vomit them back again. But if you see your pup has swallowed something, and is looking a little 'green about the gills' give him salt water or mustard water as suggested for poisoning, and if you're still concerned consult your vet.

Don't give your pup toys that are small enough for him to swallow, and if you're playing throwing games with him rather throw balls or sticks than small objects like stones which he may retrieve just a little too eagerly!

Also, when you give your dog a bone, give him a large shin bone that he can't swallow.

Overweight. (See page 114.)

Limping

There are several reasons why a dog may limp. He may, for example, have a thorn in his foot, a sore under his pad, arthritis or a sprained leg. A young pup that walks with a swaying motion may be needing calcium, which calcium powder or tablets will provide. However, some of the large breeds are afflicted with a serious orthopaedic condition known as hip dysplasia.

If your dog's limping persists, he should be taken to the vet for further examination. Hip dysplasia is hereditary. It involves a malformation of the bone structure in the pelvis of the dog. There is an operation which the vets can perform to alleviate the condition.

Hip dysplasia may be present, in some degree, in all dogs. The Kennel Club operate a scheme by which your vet can submit X-rays of your dog for grading. However, they cannot certify that any dog is totally free from it. Breeders should not breed from known afflicted dogs, and you should avoid buying pups from kennels that sell any of the breeds of dogs that are afflicted, unless they are highly graded.

In some overseas countries, no dog can be registered with their local Kennel Club without this certificate.

A dog with hip dysplasia should not be given too much exercise, and as he gets older and arthritis over-takes him, two aspirins a day will relieve the arthritis. Garlic helps people with arthritis, and there are dog owners who swear this helps relieve their dogs that are similarly afflicted.

Wounds

If a wound is deep, the dog should be taken to the vet to have it properly cleaned out and stitched. It can only be stitched, however, if the dog is taken to the vet within 24 hours.

You can attend to a minor wound yourself. It must be cleaned out with an antiseptic (Savlon is a good antiseptic) and a healing agent then applied. The wound must be encouraged to heal from the bottom up. If it forms a crust and dries out on the top, it may suppurate underneath and turn septic. Acriflavin emulsion, which you can get from your chemist, is an inexpensive and excellent healing agent.

Healing powders help dry out a wound and heal it quickly. But they should not be applied to a deep wound, because they cause the wound to dry and heal on the top.

Don't keep bathing your dog's wound or you will prevent it from healing properly. If it becomes swollen and tender, or turns septic, let your vet attend to it.

If your dog insists on licking his ointment off, apply

it just before a walk so that his mind is taken off it long enough for some of it to be absorbed, before he comes home and goes to work on it again. They say a dog's tongue has a healing effect—but most dogs overdo it.

Sometimes a dog may have a wound that won't heal because he bites it, or, if it is on his eye or ear, scratches at it, because he's trying to relieve the irritation. If the wound is to have a chance to heal, he will have to be protected against himself.

Your vet may put an Elizabethan collar or—believe it or not—a plastic bucket on your dog's neck. The bucket is actually more effective. Your vet will cut out the base, put holes around the base, and secure it to his collar. The bucket will be cut around the centre so that he can still see a little of what is going on around him! If the weather is very hot, you may suggest the vet puts some holes in it for a little ventilation.

He won't like it, but if you ever had plaster of Paris on a broken arm, nor did you! It's for his own good in the long run, and, without it, he'll never give his wound a chance to heal. Some dogs adjust to it pretty quickly—others rebel until it's removed.

If your dog is wounded, and the wound shows a pumping rhythm, and/or bleeds profusely, showing no sign of abating after some minutes, an artery has been cut, and your dog is in danger of bleeding to death if he doesn't receive attention from the vet immediately.

Accidents

In Cases of Emergency
1. Be careful not to get bitten.
2. Keep calm.
3. Save time.
4. Keep the dog warm.
5. See that the dog's breathing passages are clear.
6. Disturb the dog as little as possible.
7. Stop any excessive bleeding.
8. Treat your dog for shock.

1. *Be careful not to get bitten*

Don't handle your dog impulsively. In shock and pain he may bite anyone who approaches him.

2. *Keep calm*

Your calm attitude will communicate itself to your dog. Speak soothingly to him in a relaxed manner. The calmer you are, the less likely he is to bite. If you really feel you need to give him a muzzle, do this by standing behind him with a strip of tape (or, in an emergency, a stocking). Place this round his nose, tie it once very firmly under his chin, and then secure it behind his neck.

It is amazing how courageous dogs usually are in an accident when they're injured. They don't usually become hysterical unless their owners do—and this is a time when they really need their owner's calm support.

3. *Save time*

If your dog can't be handled, contact your vet immediately. If he can, without undue panic get your dog to your vet as soon as you can. Contact his surgery in advance, so that he can be expecting you.

4. *Keep the dog warm*

Cover him with a blanket until he's attended to.

5. *See that the dog's breathing passages are clear*

If your dog is unconscious, you must check that his air passages are clear by turning his head so that his tongue does not fall back into his throat, but hangs out of his mouth. Wipe away any blood, mucus, sand, etc., from the back of his throat as this will be blocking his breathing passages. His head must also be lowered, so that the blood and mucus drain from his mouth and do not go into his lungs which would, of course, kill him.

6. *Disturb the dog as little as possible*

When you lift your dog into a car, disturb him as little as possible. For instance, you can roll him gently on to a 'stretcher' made of a coat buttoned down the front, with two sticks (or broomsticks) placed inside it.

7. *Stop any excessive bleeding*

Until he receives medical attention, any severe bleeding must be abated by applying pressure to the wound. Tie a pad of cotton wool (or a petticoat, stocking or hankie, in an emergency) tightly against the wound. This must not, however, be left on for longer than 20 minutes. If within that time your dog still hasn't been attended to, release it for a minute or two, then reapply it. (While you're taking him to the vet, a plastic bag over the wound and newspaper will save your car seats.)

If a dog is so severely injured that he has no hope of recovery, the vet will suggest that he mercifully release the dog from his suffering. This is a difficult decision to make. But should a vet suggest it, I wouldn't hesitate to take his advice.

8. *Treat your dog for shock*

When an animal is shocked, his pulse rate quickens, he'll probably shiver, his blood pressure drops and the flow of his blood is inhibited. His gums are very pale— the equivalent of a person going white in the face when shocked. If your dog has had an accident, or needs medical attention, take him to the vet immediately.

A dog in this condition must be kept warm—if necessary, he should have a hot-water bottle next to him. (But this must *not* be more than body temperature or you will be drawing his blood to the surface of his skin, when you are wanting it to flow back to his brain.) The dog's head should be lowered slightly to promote the flow of blood to his brain.

Stay near him, speak soothingly to him and don't give him any alcohol. This will further inhibit the flow of his blood—which you're trying to restore to normal.

When taking him to the vet, a dog in this condition must not be allowed to walk. A dog suffering either from shock or heart failure, must be carried, this extra strain on him could cause his heart to fail completely.

Amputation

Should a dog's leg be badly injured, and have to be amputated, the dog's owner finds this very difficult to accept.

However, it is amazing how well dogs can adjust to three legs. It is better for a dog to have his leg removed than to have to carry the extra weight of a useless appendage for the rest of his life. Moreover, if he drags his useless leg, this may scrape on the ground and become injured. A dog without a fore-leg should adjust more

160

easily than one without a hind-leg. A dog depends on a hind-leg more for movement—and for scratching. And, of course, smaller dogs adjust more easily than big dogs.

No three-legged dog, however, should be allowed to become overweight. If his weight problem cannot be controlled, he should rather be put down.

Electrocution

Should your dog become electrocuted, he and any liquid he may be lying in are alive with current. A dog that is electrocuted may urinate, so take care not to step near him or touch him until you have both turned off the current *and* taken out the plug.

Turn his head to the side, so that his tongue does not block his breathing passages and, if he has stopped breathing, you may be able to revive him with artificial respiration if you have found him in time. If there is any sign of a pulse, you will still have some hope of reviving him. You apply artificial respiration to a dog as you do to a person.

Burns

Ice blocks or cold water placed instantly on to the burnt area will prevent any further damage to the burnt tissues and help relieve the pain. If the burn is bad, the dog should be taken to the vet immediately. Cover the burnt area with a wet cloth while you take him to the vet. When a dog is badly burnt, the whole skin on the burnt area will come away.

Heat-stroke

A dog won't suffer heat-stroke unless he has no access to shade, or is closed in a car in the direct sun for any length of time. Should this happen, however, the dog must be helped to return to normal temperature as quickly as possible, dumping it in a bath full of ice

161

would be ideal, a bucket of cold water better than nothing.

However, some dogs feel the heat more than others— *Alsatians, Keeshonds, Chows, Pugs, Bulldogs, Huskies* and *St. Bernards*, for instance. If the weather is particularly hot and your dog is uncomfortable in the heat, pour water over him to cool him—he'll love it!

Convulsions

A dog that takes a convulsion may be poisoned, be having a heart attack, he may have distemper, a bad infestation of worms, epilepsy, he may be suffering from a disturbed mental condition, or, if the dog is a bitch with puppies, she may have a calcium deficiency—a condition known as eclampsia. Your vet can diagnose the condition for you, and administer drugs (or, in the case of eclampsia, calcium injections).

If the cause of the convulsions is distress or strain (fear, loneliness, or nervousness, for example) and cannot be remedied, the dog should rather be put down.

When a dog goes into a convulsion, contact your vet immediately. This is one contingency when your vet should come *to* your dog. Your dog should not be disturbed.

Poison

One or more of the symptoms of poisoning are: extreme diarrhoea, extreme salivation, vomiting, trembling and convulsions.

Some bulbs and plants and many household products can be poisonous, but there are two main types of poisoning that a dog is likely to encounter: insecticides and poisons for vermin, such as Warfarin.

Insecticides and some chemicals may be absorbed through the skin. Other poisons may be swallowed. If poison causes the dog to go into convulsions, the vet should be summoned right away. If the cause of the poisoning is known, he must be told on the phone. If an antidote is recommended on the container, the vet must be told of the details. Pour a strong solution of salt water or mustard water down your dog's throat to make him vomit.

Strychnine

If a dog has been poisoned with strychnine, he only goes into a convulsion when he's touched or stimulated in any way. The poison itself does not kill the dog but the spasm that prevents his breathing does. For this reason it is essential that the dog is not handled, but that the vet is summoned to you. He will give the dog an anaesthetic which will relax the muscles and allow the breathing to continue. Strychnine poisoning is recognized by the way the dog becomes rigid as soon as he is touched. The less you touch your dog until the vet arrives, the better chance he has of survival.

Bee Stings

The most likely place for a dog to be stung is in his mouth while he's biting a bee buzzing about him, or sniffing and licking one that's crawling on the ground. Most dogs swell in the area that's been stung, perhaps develop a slight fever, and then it's all over.

If he'll let you, you can try to locate the sting and remove it. An aspirin is the best relief you can give him. If he swells badly and has difficulty in breathing, the vet should give him treatment.

Coughing

A dog that coughs may have, for instance, a heart condition, a throat infection, an obstruction in his throat

or worms. If the coughing persists, the vet will diagnose and treat his condition. In an old dog, coughing probably indicates a heart complaint, and treatment will give him relief—and a longer life-span. (See further under elderly dogs.)

Anal glands

Every dog has a pair of anal glands at the base of his tail. If they become congested, he will rub his bottom on the ground to relieve the irritation. In most cases, this is effective, but from time to time the congestion becomes chronic, and unless the vet squeezes them out for him, abscesses may form. Chronically infected anal glands can cause a dog's condition to become generally run down.

A dog that skates his bottom on the ground may also have tapeworms.

Phantom Pregnancy

Many bitches, although they've never been mated, develop a mild phantom pregnancy after each season. This manifests itself in a swelling of her teats, which may produce a little milk. If they become tender, massage them gently with a little olive oil. The condition usually disappears and there's no need for concern. But if, together with the swollen teats and milk your bitch frantically tries to make a nest to whelp in, and tries to find something to 'mother', she should be taken to the vet for a hormone injection, otherwise she can develop pyometra, which is very serious. A bitch suffering from phantom pregnancy can become very anxious and unhappy. Give her plenty of attention, games and walks to help her over her condition.

Oversexed Male Dogs

Dogs that seem to be constantly stimulated may have an infected prostate gland. They may also just be oversexed—and mating them makes them worse. A hormone injection from the vet is a satisfactory solution to this problem, and the kindest to the dog.

Castration

Some vets are reluctant to castrate dogs. Castration doesn't always stop a dog biting and fighting—although, if he is roaming in search of romance, it will help to keep him at home. If he is roaming because he's bored, it will, of course, make no difference.

Every dog that I've seen after castration has maintained his figure and has been affected in no adverse way. Sometimes, however, a dog may become fat and lose some of his vitality. Whenever a dog is castrated, care should be taken that he doesn't put on weight.

Discharge

Most male dogs have a slight discharge from the sheath—especially at puberty. This is normal, and need cause no concern. But if it becomes copious and smells offensive, there is an infection, and the dog should be taken to the vet.

Dull Coat

A dull coat on a dog may mean that your dog needs more fat in his diet (milk or a tablespoon or two of sunflower oil on his food will supply this) or he may be out of condition. Lack of exercise, worms or obesity can all cause a dog to be out of condition. His coat may be full of loose hair, and a brushing may make him shine again. He may be needing a bath—or his coat may be dull and dry from *too* much bathing, particularly if he's bathed with a strong soap. If the dog is a spayed bitch, she may have a hormone deficiency—the vet will diagnose this for you.

A clean healthy dog, free of worms, that gets plenty of exercise, a balanced diet and a regular brushing should always have a nice glossy coat.

White Flakes

This dandruff-like appearance in a dog's coat is rather like dandruff in people, and an antidandruff shampoo should clear it up.

Bad Breath

A dog that has a bad breath may have worms. He could also have bad teeth, be needing more exercise, and needing a better balanced diet. He may have a mouth or throat infection, an upset stomach, or maybe he's eaten something rotten.

If your dog is in good health and still doesn't have a

166

clean breath, Amplex tablets will help make him 'nice to be near'. These can be obtained from your chemist.

Doggy Odours

A smelly dog in the house is not pleasant. But it's not too much trouble to keep a dog free of odour.

Some dogs are more prone to odour than others. One dog will need to be bathed twice a month in some sweet-smelling shampoo if he's not to have his presence detected two blocks away; another no more than once in six months. Some dogs must be brushed at least twice a week to keep their odour down; others never.

An older dog may become more odorous and Amplex pills, administered as suggested on the package (obtainable from chemists) will help control this. If a dog has eczema, he will also have a strong smell. (See ahead for curing eczema.)

If a dog excretes a urinous smell from his skin, his kidneys are not functioning properly and he needs veterinary attention. There are pills which will relieve this condition immediately. (See further under elderly dogs.)

Flatulence

Old dogs can make family gatherings around the fire rather unpleasant. When your dog starts blowing under the table, striking a match will clear the air immediately. Medical charcoal tablets, for human consumption, are very effective in absorbing the gases in a dog's stomach. One tablet should last quite some time. Wrap it up in butter and your dog won't even know he's had such a revolting pill!

Medical charcoal can be bought from the chemist.

A change in diet may also relieve a dog's flatulence.

Rashes

Mild rashes can be cured with a sulphur-based ointment. Eczema and allergies are dealt with below.

Ringworm

Ringworm is detected by small round patches of hair falling out, or becoming loose and broken. Unlike ringworm in cats, it is not readily transferred to humans. Ringworm (in both cats *and* dogs) is easily cured by pills which you can get from your vet.

Excessive Scratching and Eczema

Your dog may be scratching because he needs a bath, because he has fleas, a slight skin irritation or an allergy. Your dog may have a hormone imbalance, a fungal infection, mange. There may be any one of a number of reasons, which your vet may diagnose for you.

A temporary and slight irritation can be cleared up with an ointment such as Valderma, or Germolene, or Dettol—which will also give your dog temporary relief from a more serious skin condition—while the condition is being treated.

If your dog only scratches in excessively hot weather, pour a bucket of cold water over him, and he'll enjoy the relief from the heat, or it may be a compulsive type of scratching as described earlier.

Eczema is a very comprehensive term covering many different forms of skin ailments in dogs, the causes of which are varied and may be difficult to determine.

If your dog has eczema, first and foremost see that he doesn't have even one flea on him. Just as some people are allergic to bee stings or mosquito bites, so are some dogs allergic to a flea bite, breaking out in large inflamed areas, usually around the base of the tail. The dog bites the area continuously, making the irritation worse, and his hair will probably start falling out, but once the fleas have been cleared your dog's coat will return to normal.

Vets usually give cortisone injections or antihistamine pills to relieve the irritation. But the only way to give a dog permanent relief is to keep him completely free of fleas.

However, if you're sending your dog to kennels, he should get a cortisone injection before he goes, to prevent the irritation starting up again while he is in kennels.

Cortisone is not harmful to a dog, except—as with people who are on cortisone—in the event of an accident. Then the vet treating the dog must be told that the dog is on cortisone injections.

If ridding your dog of fleas does not stop his scratching, he may have some other allergy. Some dogs are allergic to household dust, for instance. This usually manifests itself in small pimple-like outbursts around the dog's chest and legs, where he rests on the ground. This is, as with allergies in people, very difficult to eradicate. A cream with a sulphur base which your chemist can supply, or a cream which your vet may prescribe, will give him relief.

We are what we eat. It makes sense, therefore, that if a dog is getting the wrong food he won't be well. This may manifest itself in skin troubles. A number of people have told me that after putting a dog on a different diet their dog's eczema has cleared up. This is mostly the case with small dogs that are getting too rich a diet. If the dog is on balanced rations, the rations may have to be diluted with vegetables and wholewheat bread. Some dogs can't take too much protein.

Your dog may also have a form of mange, which a skin scraping, done by your vet, can determine. Whatever treatment he prescribes, be careful to follow his instructions exactly as he advises.

Convalescence

If your dog is convalescing from an illness or injury, he'll probably want you near him as much as possible.

Provided he is not *too* ill, and that you give him proper care and that your vet permits this, it is better for him to convalesce at home, rather than at kennels or at a veterinary hospital.

Give him reassurance, keep calm, and don't be away from him for long intervals. Keep him warm, since he's not moving about much, and keep him out of a draught — but keep the room well ventilated and do not over-heat it.

Other animals and children should be kept away from him.

Take him out to relieve himself every four hours, or so, supporting him carefully, if necessary, and consult your vet about any special diet he may need. (See under diet.) Keep fresh water near him at all times. If he won't drink, you may have to spoon some into his mouth, as described for administering liquids. If he's too weak to eat, try to tempt him with a little Marmite or chicken essence, prompting him to eat by putting a little on his nose once or twice, to see if he'll take it. If he will drink milk, put some Complan in it. This is a complete food, and an excellent invalid diet. It is available from chemists.

If your dog doesn't start eating within a day or two, you must take him back to your vet.

Deafness

Some dogs are born deaf (some white *Bull Terriers* and some white *Boxers* for example) and some dogs become deaf with old age.

It can be a big problem caring for a deaf dog that's young and full of life. He can't be called, and therefore can't be controlled. If his owner cannot give him adequate care, he should rather be put down than letting him cause a lot of trouble and anxiety and risk being run over or causing an accident.

An old dog, on the other hand, knows the ways of his owners and leads a quiet life. He may even have learnt to respond to vibrations. He should, of course, be given extra care, because he can't look after himself the way he used to. And because he can't be called, he should never be exercised where there's any danger of traffic.

Blindness

Once again, it's easier for an old dog to adjust to blindness than it is for a young dog that may suddenly be prevented from leading a very active and full life.

If you have a blind dog, don't leave him alone too much, don't rearrange furniture (so that he can find his way around), and keep him off the streets. (If a dog has lost only one eye, and knows his way around the streets, it can also be dangerous being able to see on only one side.) Whether to allow him to continue to live or not depends on whether or not he is happy. If his life is obviously a hardship, it is kinder to put him down, but because a dog depends so much on his sense of smell he should adjust quite well. Once again, a blind dog will need that extra care and companionship.

Care of the Elderly Dog

An old dog has a charm and dignity all his own.

Some dogs age quicker than others. Generally speaking, large dogs age sooner than small ones. And, without doubt, the more exercise they've had, the later they will age.

An old dog needs much more peace and sleep than a young dog does—he will really appreciate a comfortable bed or basket that is always accessible to him.

If you are considering getting a new pup before he goes, see page 45 on the section on choosing a dog to replace an old dog, before making the decision.

Don't let an old dog get over-tired—reduce his exercise as you see fit. His heart can't take the strain it used to. However, to keep an old dog young at heart and interested in life, give him outings, and play with him whenever he asks for a game—without, of course, over-tiring him.

If your dog is not eating well, a daily multivitamin pill will supply the vitamins he's not getting. There are also preparations on the market which your vet may prescribe. These preparations will relieve the symptoms of senility, and will give your dog added vigour.

When dogs get old, they become prone to both heart and kidney trouble. Heart attacks are very rare in dogs, but a dog may, for instance, have a leaking valve. Heart trouble will manifest itself in shortage of breath, coughing attacks, and spasms similar to an asthma attack. The dog's legs and abdomen may also swell, becoming puffy with the accumulation of fluid.

Your vet can give your dog relief with pills that will give him a new lease of life and make him feel 'like a new dog'! You'll probably feel like a new dog, too!

A dog that is being treated for a heart condition must be given a completely salt-free diet. This will involve taking him off his balanced ration and cooking meat, vegetables and porridge for him—without the addition of any salt. This will immediately alleviate the heart condition. Any pre-prepared food like balanced ration, bread, and so on, do, of course contain salt.

A kidney condition manifests itself, firstly, by a dog's excessive thirst. Your dog may also excrete urine from his skin which you will detect by its odour.

Any elderly dog that starts drinking water more frequently than usual should always be taken to the vet.

There is treatment available which will help your dog's kidneys function properly again, give him relief, pick up his condition and give him new vigour.

A dog with a chronic kidney complaint must always have ample fresh water available 24 hours of the day. His protein intake should also be reduced, and your vet may suggest a little bicarbonate of soda in his water if his urine is acid. But don't put *too* much in, or his body will overcompensate and his urine will become *more* acid.

Whatever treatment your dog is getting from your vet, follow his directions carefully.

The End of the Road

None of us would like to see our dogs outlive us, with no-one to care for them—it's this that makes it easier to say goodbye to them, together with the knowledge that we've given them all those years of happiness. When your dog's life becomes a hardship, and brings him no pleasure, show him the courage and loyalty he has shown you over the years. He has to go sometime in the near future and looks to you to spare him needless pain, lameness and discomfort he surely doesn't deserve, and can so easily be spared.

Your vet will know your dog after all the years he's attended to him, and will appreciate your desire to let his end be peaceful and free from fear. A visit to your home, and an injection, and your dog is eased painlessly into the place where all good doggies go.

Try not to let your dog see you show any distress, and if you really can't bring yourself to do it, perhaps a kind friend will do it for you. If you are with your dog, soothing him while he gets his anaesthetic, you will have the knowledge for the rest of your life that he went in peace without any fear.

It is wise to ask your vet to dispose of the body. If you bury it in your garden, there is probably going to be a newcomer, or there will be visiting dogs and children digging in the garden—and it will also help you not to brood over it if the vet attends to it for you.

CHAPTER 6

KENNELLING AND TRAVELLING WITH YOUR DOG

Kennelling

Most dogs settle down surprisingly well in kennels—provided the kennel is properly run, or that they're not doing too long a stretch.

Do not take your dog to any kennel unless you've inspected the conditions thoroughly, and ascertained that the dogs are fed *every* day. The condition of the dogs in the kennels, the appearance of the water-dishes, the absence of stools, odour and flies, all reveal the way the place is run. Also observe, if you can, how those in attendance at the kennels handle the dogs, because a frightening experience can have a permanent effect on your dog. Genuine affection for the inmates, and an impatient or offhand manner are not too difficult to distinguish.

If the owners of any kennels won't allow you to inspect their premises, don't consider leaving your pet there. If the place is well run they'll be proud to show you around.

There should always be a closed-in area where dogs can be caught, should they get out of their kennel.

You may like to settle your dog in his kennel yourself, perhaps bringing his own bedding along, so that he'll be more comfortable. Not many kennels provide comfortable bedding because of the extra work and expense.

If you also leave an old shoe or ball which smells of you, and which gives your dog something to play with, it may also help him to settle down.

Unless the visit is daily, I don't, under normal circumstances, think dogs should be visited by their owners while they're in kennels for short spells—when they are in season, for instance. They get used to the routine and bustle of the kennels, and when you come they obviously think they're going home with you, are dejected at being left once more and have to settle down all over again. However, if a dog is in for a long time, he certainly may be visited—as often as possible. If he's in for so long, the visits themselves become part of his routine.

And finally, book your dog in the kennel of your choice as early as you possibly can; give the kennels your holiday address—and forget about him. Worrying isn't going to help him. If anything's wrong, you'll hear from the kennels. He's probably having as good a holiday as you!

Travelling and your Dog

If you're thinking of travelling with your dog, find out well in advance which hotels, motels, caravan parks and so on will allow you to bring him with you. (If the dogs they allow are clean and behave nicely—they won't quickly change their policy about allowing animals into their premises in future—and others will benefit!)

(a) By car

Put your name, address and phone number on your dog's collar, and if he's travelling a long distance write on his collar: 'Return to police station if found.' It's not likely that your dog will get lost—but it's happened before. And if it does happen, he may be traced to the nearest police station where he was last seen.

Take water for your dog and give him as many breaks

175

in the journey as you can—for a run, a drink and to relieve himself. When you stop for a break, always keep him on a lead. Apart from the dangers of being lost or run over, no one relishes the picture of wanting to get on with the journey while Rover still has a rabbit or two to catch!

If it's hot, he will also appreciate a slightly open window for fresh air, but not wide enough for him to lean out of.

If your dog doesn't like travelling, your vet can prescribe some tranquillizers for him.

(See further on car outings in chapter 3.)

(b) By Rail or Air

Don't trust either letter or telegram with instructions regarding the arrival of your dog to whoever is meeting him. Telephone them personally, and *know* that he'll be met on time. For obvious reasons, don't arrange for anyone you don't personally know and trust to meet him.

Take your dog to the airport or station yourself, and put him into his box at the last possible moment (if he's to fly). Some pet agencies take the whole day's 'consignment' along together, whether they are to leave in one or eight hours. You don't want this happening to your dog. You will also find it's much cheaper to do it yourself.

If you're buying a new dog, never buy him without seeing him first. If you buy him through an advertisement and have him railed or flown to you, you can easily be misled—as so often happens. Then you'll probably be too sorry for the pup to send him back, so that you're landed with a dog you didn't really want.

If you're spending so much money on him, and are hoping to own him for ten to fifteen years, it's worth the trip to choose and fetch him yourself. Then not only are you certain of having the dog you chose and paid for but you have not risked spoiling his temperament.

Quite a few dogs that have had this experience have been brought to me for nervousness, and they have never regained their former confidence.

(c) By rail

Accompanied dogs are allowed into train compartments with their owners on British Rail provided that no other passenger objects. They have to have a ticket which is half the full fare. Unaccompanied dogs are only accepted at certain designated stations and a list of these can be obtained from British Rail, who also issue a leaflet on the labelling and crating of livestock.

(d) By air

If your dog is to travel by air, he will need a crate. Airway regulations require that this is large enough for him to stand up and turn around in. Don't guess — measure your dog and his crate carefully. An animal transport agency will supply you with a crate of the correct size. You must be sure that the box is of the correct dimensions and strong enough to contain your dog — especially if he is of a large breed. Those strong jaws can get through a lot of crating once they get busy!

Ventilation must be supplied on *all six* sides. Dogs have been known to suffocate while sleeping under sedation, because there was only ventilation at the top.

The labels must be placed very securely on the crate.

Let your dog get used to his crate for some days before he travels. You can even turn it on its side with his bedding in it, so that he gets used to sleeping in it for a few days before he is due to fly.

If your dog is to travel overseas, each country has its own regulations regarding inoculations, travelling specifications and so on. Some countries don't allow dogs in, others quarantine them for six months and with others there is no problem. The airways all have a list of these specifications. These regulations must be strictly adhered to, because they are for your own protection, as well as for the protection of the country that enforces them. People who try to evade health regulations can inadvertently introduce a serious epidemic into a country.

CHAPTER 7

CORRECTION AND REWARD IN THE ADULT DOG

In the introduction to the chapter on puppy discipline, the subject of correcting and rewarding your dog is discussed. However, now that he's fully grown and ready to be trained, we'll go into this subject more fully. But to avoid too much repetition, I would suggest that you refer to that section of the book as well.

(a) Rewards

You say 'good dog':
(1) when your dog has obeyed you;
(2) when he hesitates and your reward tips the balance of his indecision;
(3) when you need to restore your dog's trust in you.

Now, let's discuss each in turn.

(1) *You say 'good dog' when your dog has obeyed you*

You do this, firstly, to indicate to him that he has done the right thing; secondly, to repay him, making it worth his while to obey you; and thirdly, to add incentive to further obedience. If he gets a reward he thoroughly enjoys, he'll be that much more willing to obey you next time.

When do you reward him? You reward your dog every time he obeys you, the *very instant* he obeys—even before he has actually decided that he *is* going to obey you.

How do you reward him? James Kinney said in his book *The Town Dog*: 'The dog will learn for nothing more tangible than a kind word and a pat on the head, which convinces us, of course, that the dog is a fool.'

Never reward your dog with food. He must obey you for the pleasure he derives from your display of approval, and not for his own selfish motives. Rewarding a dog with food is fairly widely practised because of the little effort it requires, but when a dog starts expecting food his responses become mechanical; he doesn't obey with the same zest as a dog that's rewarded and stimulated with petting and praise; and if he isn't hungry . . .?

While your dog is learning, your rewards should be out of all proportion to what he's actually done. The praise you give him should be sparkling and extravagant. You can certainly *over*punish your dog, but you can't reward him too much. He's a glutton for praise—take advantage of this delightful aspect of his make-up.

This is how you reward your dog: Pat him hard and stimulate him, saying 'There's a clever dog!', 'Good *boy!*' and so on, in a spirited voice, conveying to him that you never believed he could be *so* brilliant. If, when you pat him, you bend over him so that he's near your face, he'll work even harder to earn his praise. Dull, mechanical, infrequent and half-hearted rewards don't make being obedient very exciting for a dog. (Always pat your dog on his shoulder, on his side, or the side of his head. Dogs flinch when patted exuberantly on top of their heads.)

However, if such praise *over*-excites your dog, modulate your reward to suit his temperament. Speak to him warmly, in a voice that conveys your pleasure, but doesn't overstimulate him. And instead of patting him (because he'll just jump up all over you), stroke him firmly, or, if you're doing heel work, give him a hand to sniff or lick, or just touch his head. This is quite sufficient incentive to make an excitable or willing dog work eagerly while he's being trained.

When you're training or commanding your dog, you're competing for his attention against smells, noises and other distractions. Why should any sensible dog obey commands without a reason? (Unless it's through fear.) When he's not pulling on the lead, or when he comes when he's called, etc., or whatever the command may be, give him a *reason* to walk nicely, or come . . . because he wants to earn the pleasure he derives from being patted and from hearing your display of pride and pleasure in his achievements. Your dog's not concentrating? Give him a *reason* to! In everyday situations, give him a reason for coming away from the postman and leaving the neighbour's cat in one piece. If he could speak, he should say: 'My reward was *much* more fun than chasing the cat!' The more he gave up for you, the more *you* give back to him.

When he's fully trained, a pat or a quick warm 'Good boy!' will suffice for simple commands.

(2) *When you call your dog and he hesitates*, not quite sure whether he can get away with it or not, or whether it wouldn't possibly be more fun to hare off down the road with his pals, you will probably repeat your command, and the chances are you won't see him for dust. However, should you, at the point where he hesitates, *reward* him instead of repeating your command, he is sure to come, attracted by the promise in your voice. And if you crouch down—you double your chances!

(3) *When you need to restore your dog's trust in you*

To do this, you must know how to restore his trust in you, which, naturally enough, he will lose for a moment from time to time.

When you handle an excitable dog, the success you have in bringing him under control depends on the principle that a dog must have a perfect balance of trust and fear in order to obey willingly. Some dogs are born with this balance, and give no trouble, being submissive by nature, and others have to be trained.

A dog disobeys because he has too *much* or too *little* fear of his owner. Fear is a strong word, but for our purpose, it describes an attitude or emotion in a dog indicating a strong and healthy respect for his owner. We shall use the word 'fear' in this book for want of a better. It may be an overall attitude, or it may fluctuate from time to time.

In order to bring a dog under perfect and willing control, the dog's owner must know how to adjust this attitude. If a dog is disobedient because he has too *much* fear of his owner, and is then commanded, his fear increases and he becomes *less* obedient. In other words he runs away. But if he's disobedient because he has too *little* fear of his owner, and is then commanded, he says: 'Go take a running jump, I'm enjoying myself'—and goes on enjoying himself.

How do you cancel the first dog's fear in order to make him obey, and instil the second dog with this healthy respect for his owner? This is what we shall be discussing in the next few paragraphs, because it is the very key to training a dog.

You cancel the first dog's fear by restoring his trust in you. You deal with the second situation by punishing your dog. This we'll come to a little later under 'corrections'.

Your dog may be *too scared* to come to you because you have a medicine bottle in your hand, because he's reluctant to part with a sock or have a bath, or because he's panicking, lost for a moment in a crowd or busy street. He may just have been punished, or may be reluctant to get into a car, for fear of a visit to a vet or the kennels—there are any number of reasons why your dog may be afraid to come to you. Calling or commanding him will make him more afraid, so you must 'restore trust' to get him to come to you.

This is how you restore trust:

(1) Crouch down. This diminishes your size and apparent threat to your dog, and also gives your dog tempting access to your face. But be careful with a big dog. If he's *too* tempted, you'll land flat on your back! Intercept him with an outstretched hand under his throat and stand up quickly before he reaches you. This way he can't knock you over so easily.

(2) Remain completely relaxed and confident.

(3) *Do not* take even one step towards him—if anything, step away from him.

(4) Say 'Good dog!' and speak to him warmly and convincingly.

(5) Pet him lovingly when he has voluntarily come right up to you, attracted by your tone of voice and the easy access to your face. Don't grab him. If he's very stiff-legged and cautious when he comes, tickle his tummy or behind his ears until he's more relaxed and has more confidence.

(6) Then continue gently with what you want to do— resume training, put him in the car, or whatever it may be. The degree of his fear will determine how long you need to take to soothe him.

It is essential that you keep relaxed. Don't be in a hurry, and make no attempt whatever to catch him. Keep your hands close to yourself, letting your dog seek them, then use them only to pet him with until he's confident again.

To win the confidence of a nervous or apprehensive dog in this way is far easier than you would ever expect.

When you restore trust, however, you may simply need to follow point (4) alone or points (1), (2), (3) and (4), depending on the degree of your dog's anxiety.

Never take advantage of the fact that your dog will come to you if you restore trust. For instance, if he's just chewed your new plant and won't admit it—don't draw him to you by saying 'Good boy!' smoothly, then clobber him across the chops when he comes!

(b) Corrections

The effectiveness of a punishment is determined not by what you *do* to your dog, but by what your dog *feels*. Two different dogs can feel exactly the same degree of distress when one is simply told 'Bad dog!' and the other is hit hard with a stick.

Just as you must adjust your reward to suit your dog's temperament, so must you adjust your correction.

(1) *How should you correct your dog?*

This depends on the circumstances, whether he's on a lead or not, whether he's within reach, how naughty he's been, his age and temperament, and your strength. Chapter 2 on Puppy Discipline, and further chapters on training your dog, give you guidance on how best to correct your dog under various circumstances.

(2) *How does correction work?*

Your dog is disobedient because he doesn't need you at that particular moment. He's enjoying himself, and can manage very nicely without you, thank you! So you punish him, and upset him. You then offer him the refuge that *you* made him need. You do this by restoring trust, which (if you do it correctly) will bring him to you immediately.

If you say: 'That serves you right!', using punishment purely for personal revenge, or, after the punishment, *command* him to come to you, you're not making full use of your correction, and your dog will either become scared of you or independent of you. It's simple: make him need you—then give him what *you* made him need. When he's learnt, he'll short-cut the correction, and come for his reward.

(3) *How much should you correct your dog?*

In the first paragraph on correction, we established that every dog has a different threshold of punishment. You must calculate your own dog's threshold. You must not punish above this threshold and terrify him, nor must you repeatedly punish below it. If, although your dog finds his correction worth avoiding, he still comes readily to you when you restore trust, you have correctly established your dog's threshold of punishment.

However, while deciding how heavily you should correct him, rather err on the light side. Should you lose your dog's confidence you may not regain it.

A gentle and willing dog will simply need a verbal reprimand, but a stubborn, boisterous and excitable dog will need physical correction. If your dog tries to dodge his punishment, or if he continues to commit his crimes in spite of repeated corrections, your correction is too light and you are not reaching his threshold—provided, that is, that your demands are reasonable. (See ahead.) Repeatedly underpunishing a dog has the effect of making him sly, or independent of you. Some dogs even bite their owners when they are corrected too lightly.

In the long run, it is cruel to punish a dog too lightly. This is, firstly, because he'll be getting repeated corrections; secondly, because he's missing out on all the rewards he would otherwise be getting when avoiding his wholesome punishments, and thereby being obedient; and thirdly, because he may become so unmanageable that he's always being locked outside or, worse, passes from home to home or has to be put down because no one wants him simply because no one has dared to punish him properly.

. . . punish below it . . .

Pain lasting a couple of seconds is a small price to pay for a lifetime of harmony. So be kind to your dog and make his corrections worth avoiding.

Some people don't like correcting their dog properly because they are afraid their dog may turn into a cringing animal. But if a dog is not *over*corrected, if he always receives adequate praise, and his owner always restores trust after correcting him, this won't happen.

However, with some very tough dogs, cringing is a necessary phase in a successful training programme. It indicates that the dog is beginning to learn. When a dog cringes, his trainer should then, instead of correcting him further—restore trust, and should now give him abundant praise, handling his dog *lightly*. The dog, now carefully avoiding his punishments, obeys in a cringing manner. As he begins to enjoy his rewards and regains his confidence, he realizes that it's nice, after all, to be good. The cringing then disappears, and the dog now obeys willingly. He may still need an occasional punishment, but this should be much lighter, as he is now under control.

It is not every dog, however, that goes through this cringing phase during training. If a willing dog cringes, there's something very wrong with the way he's being handled. It is only a tough, calculating dog that may show this reaction during training, and it shouldn't last more than a few lessons. A willing dog that cringes is usually being handled in a domineering manner, which is undesirable and offensive to witness.

When you punish your dog, always make it clear to him whether he's being punished for disobeying a command, or for doing something in particular which is forbidden. For example, if he's barking, only punish him if he continues to do so *after* he has been commanded to stop. But *whenever* he sniffs up dresses, he's clobbered.

(4) *Reasons for a dog being disobedient, despite repeated corrections*

If you find yourself repeatedly correcting your dog without his showing any signs of becoming more obedient:

(i) The demands made on him may be too much. He may, for example, be repeatedly and perfectly adequately punished for digging in the garden, but he's not getting enough exercise. Or he may be punished for jumping up, but he's not getting enough attention or companionship.

(ii) He may not understand. What you're trying to teach him may be beyond him, or your instructions not clear enough.

(iii) Your corrections may be too light.

(iv) You may be inconsistent. You may be allowing him to get away with something sometimes, and punishing him on other occasions.

(v) The temptation may be too much for him—if he's punished for stealing Kitty's meat left on the floor, or jumping a fence when he sees all his pals outside for example.

(vi) You may be showing him too little authority; pleading with him or shouting at him instead of commanding him.

(vii) Perhaps you're not making it worth his while to be good.

(viii) Perhaps the only time he ever gets notice taken of him is when he's naughty!

(5) *Why do people so often undercorrect their dog?*

People may undercorrect their dogs for a number of reasons. They either don't want them to cringe (this only becomes chronic if the dog is very nervous or is being overpunished); or they don't want to break their dog's spirit (highly unlikely in a spirited dog); they've been told it's wrong (many misguided dog lovers tell people never to hit their dog, and many dogs thereby lose a home when they get out of hand); they feel uncivilized and barbaric (understandable); they are afraid of their dog (this dog should be professionally trained, given to someone who can handle him, or put down); they wouldn't hit their child, so how can they hit their dog? (a big strong dog isn't a child); they feel sorry for the dog (he gets over it quicker than you think).

A dog's threshold of punishment, however, is not static. For example, he'll jump out of his skin if you smack him while he's sleeping, but he won't even notice it if you do it to him in a dog-fight. These two examples are at opposite ends of the extremities you're likely to encounter. Your dog will take a heavier correction when there are other dogs running around distracting him than he will under quiet training conditions. What is important for the punishment to be effective, though, is that *it exceeds the intensity of the excitement* created by the situation. A dog is tough, and if he's barking furiously or chasing a cat, he won't even notice a correction, unless it exceeds the intensity of this excitement. Under such conditions, his pain threshold is surprisingly high.

Your corrections should become less intense and less frequent as your dog becomes more obedient.

(c) Conclusion

Your dog's ancestors were social animals and therefore lived in packs. Because your dog has inherited this need for companionship, he adapts readily to domestication. He has also inherited a need for a leader. The pack leader had (and still has, among wild dogs) an instinct to dominate the dogs in the pack, keeping them fed, safe and disciplined. The average dog in the pack has a complimentary instinct to be submissive to his pack leader. If he's not submissive, the pack leader bullies him until he is—the equivalent of our training.

You can fulfil your dog's need for a pack leader by showing him authority—he'll love you far more if you do. Don't we all remember how much more pleasure we got from a word of praise given us by a teacher that was strict?

Dogs are no longer set to fight badgers and bears and one another. Nor are they left half starved on the end of a chain as a matter of course all their lives. But the pendulum has swung the other way, and they have been elevated to almost more than human level.

Look at the way a large, tough dog comes out of a fight, head held high, with a wag of his tail and a gleam in his eye, absolutely exhilarated—possibly bleeding from a dozen or more wounds. He may even come out of this combat with his opponent, who has powerful jaws and massive fangs—completely unscathed . . . yet we hesitate to lift a manicured hand to his tough hide and skull! And what happens? The owners of these powerful dogs are heartbroken because they cannot control them. Let's look at them for what they really are, and treat them accordingly.

Once again, I'm not talking about dogs with a gentle spirit, because they're not the victims of over-sentimentalism.

CHAPTER 8

WHY TRAIN YOUR DOG?

Why train your dog? Train him because he's intelligent and capable of learning *so* much—that's one very good reason for training him. And if he's disobedient, that's another very good reason for training him. It's certainly worth a try, and you may find you and your dog very proud of what you've achieved together.

It's amazing what dogs can learn. Dogs know more about their owners than their owners ever dream of. They have a considerable passive vocabulary (that goes without saying of course!); just because they can't talk, we think they can't understand. A dog's mind isn't full of thoughts of finance and household matters, plans for the future, and so on; so when he's not snoozing or thinking about the dog next door, he's probably busy anticipating your next move—particularly if it signifies an outing or his next meal. A slight change in routine or a different inflection in your voice, for instance, tell him all sorts of things, like whether he's due for a ride in the car, or a visit to the kennels, or whether it's walk or bath time for him. And many a family has noticed how their dog can pick out a number of words in ordinary conversation.

Where *would* we be without dogs? Besides the large contribution they make to the economy of the country with the production of foodstuffs etc., and the employment they provide for thousands, their intelligent brains are put to full use as sheep, guard, police, war, rescue, sledge, hunting and guide dogs. They round up stray sheep in the hills and lead herds over long distances, track down criminals, detect drugs, lead the blind, find lost children, locate victims of bomb blasts, avalanches and earthquakes. In so many spheres of life, the services dogs render are indispensable, to say nothing of the unequalled loyalty and companionship they give to millions of otherwise very lonely people—and the protection and security they provide so many families.

The police could never be without their dogs. One dog in the Australian Police Force had a vocabulary of over 400 words. Amongst other feats, she could be ordered to turn taps on and off, fill buckets with water, walk down ladders frontwards and backwards, take off her collar and, so they say, put it back—*and* she could obey these commands equally well when they were given via a transmitter strapped to her back! (*Dogs that serve* by L. G. Cashmore, published by George Ronald, London.)

Alsatians in Austria rescuing injured climbers in the Alps or people buried by avalanches can locate victims buried as deep as 2 metres in the snow. These dogs go out in threes, and when they find someone buried they dig him out. One licks his face to revive him, another warms him by lying on him, while the third summons help. They are even taught to use any ski tracks that may be available, because the snow is packed hard in these and this conserves their strength for the long distances they have to run.

Why train your dog? Train him because he deserves it and because he is capable of learning *so* much!

CHAPTER 9

GENERAL RULES
FOR TRAINING A DOG

Before attempting to train your dog, refer to the section on choosing a dog to train, for guidance as to how various breeds react when being trained and adapt your instructions on training your dog wherever necessary.

1. Unless your dog is quite out of hand and desperately needs to be trained, don't begin his formal training until he's fully mature. He's mature enough to be trained when he's no longer floppy and uncoordinated. Small dogs mature at about five to six months, and giant breeds

when they're about fifteen months old. Labradors and dogs of that size are usually co-ordinated enough when they're about seven to nine months old. If, when you press your dog's hindquarters gently, his back legs are strong enough to resist you—he should be ready for training. But if he hasn't the strength in his legs, and sways or collapses, don't train him yet. If you try to start training a dog too early, you may confuse him and spoil him for training for the rest of his life.

On the other hand, most dogs can begin their formal training at any age up to about six years old or more. If your dog's older than that, and gets plenty of exercise, can still hear well, has bright eyes and runs around a lot, he can still learn. You *can* teach an old dog new tricks! If the dog you are training is no longer young, use a light correction, go slowly, and give him ample reward. Don't strain him and, unless he enjoys his lessons, don't train him.

2. Use the following equipment:

(*a*) A metre lead. Many people find a longer one clumsy to handle. Use only the type shown in the illustration; lighter leads are not strong enough, and if you use a metal one you won't be able to adjust your correction accurately.

(*b*) A check chain that fits properly. When it tightens on your dog's neck, 13 centimetres should protrude from the ring. With the connection against the right side of his neck, the loose end of the chain should slide up and not down.

A check chain is not cruel. A dog's neck is muscular and therefore he cannot be easily strangled. Small children shouldn't have access to these chains—they can be dangerous.

This training equipment can be a Chinese puzzle to novices because the rings can't be joined or separated. To make a noose, hold your chain vertically, one ring in each hand. Hold the bottom ring horizontally and lower the top ring, letting the chain slide through the bottom ring until you have a noose.

Rare is the dog that obligingly slips his head through a check chain that's presented to him. If your dog resists when you try to put it on him, handle him thus: kneel in front of him and pet him in a relaxed and loving manner. Slip your left arm into the check chain. Keep the chain as far as possible out of his sight. After stroking his head with your left hand for a few seconds, sneak the chain over his head with your right hand. If he jerks his head up, grab a handful of loose skin under his chin to keep his head down, while you slip the chain over. If he jerks his head down, grab some skin at the top of his neck to hold his head up—if necessary, lifting his front legs off the ground. Pet him warmly once it's on.

If he bucks and tries to get free as soon as it's on him, quickly draw the chain tight and hold the lead short. Then pet him lovingly to regain his confidence, and as he gains confidence loosen your hold gradually. (See the chapter on problem dogs for dogs that refuse to accept a lead.)

Some dogs never co-operate in having their chains put on—sometimes for the simple reason that they're too eager to get on with their lesson! And some of them can be so crafty about it!

While you're training your dog, the check chain should be loose *at all times* (except during a correction, whereafter it should slacken immediately). It will be necessary from time to time during a lesson to adjust its position so that you're not working with it wrapped around your dog's neck, but hanging loose with the connection in front of him or just above his right shoulder.

3. When you approach your training area, convey to your dog that he's about to enjoy himself. Don't proceed as quickly as you can, anxious to get started and eager to get results. As far as your dog's concerned, he's going for pleasure.

4. *Keep relaxed while you train.* If you find yourself getting tense, pause and relax, or terminate the lesson at that point. Resume training only when you can do so in a completely relaxed manner. A dog finds it easy to work with a relaxed, calm (but, if necessary—still very firm) handler, but he quickly picks up his handler's tension.

5. Train your dog in a cool, adequately spacious area, with water at half-time if necessary. If your dog is hot, pour water over his coat and work in the shade. Don't train your dog in the direct sun on a hot day. Keep your training sessions for early morning or the late afternoon in midsummer.

6. Don't train your dog if he's tired (after a game or a run, for instance), off colour, in season (in the case of bitches) or hungry. Be sure that he's had an opportunity to relieve himself before each lesson.

7. Never attempt to proceed with a lesson if your dog has just done something to irritate you, or if you don't feel well. Illness setting in, the morning after the night before, tiredness, irritation with the dog or frustration over some private matter, will all have an adverse affect on the results of your training. If you miss several lessons under these circumstances—you'll achieve better results in the long run.

What you correctly teach a dog, he will never ever forget!

8. Don't train your dog with high heels, flapping coat, tight skirt, sunglasses or with a cigarette in your hand.

9. Until your dog's lessons are advanced, don't train him while he has more important matters on his mind. Wait until he's familiar with the smells in the area—training is difficult enough without competing against unnecessary distractions. Start training your dog under quiet conditions, and work *gradually* to where he is able to work against distractions.

10. When something distracts your dog don't give up in despair. Simply make your commands more forceful, your rewards more exciting and your punishments sharper.

11. Reward *every single* command which he obeys and punish him *each time* he disobeys. This cannot be emphasized enough. Aim at this ideal, and your dog will respect you, concentrate better, enjoy his lessons more, and become an obedient and well-trained dog in a surprisingly short time. Reward every command he obeys. Punish every command he disobeys. This is the key to successful training.

12. Before each lesson, take time to tune in to your dog.

If he is anxious, win his confidence completely. (See point 24 below.) If he is distracted or indifferent, stimulate him. If he refuses to show any interest in you, step away from him—he won't want to be separated from you, so he'll keep a better eye on you. Start only when you have his full attention.

If he's over-excited calm him down. To do this, stand close to him and handle him in a firm, decisive, positive manner. You *must* be relaxed—if you're angry or frustrated, you'll excite him further. Pet him soothingly, but *firmly*, with both hands, speaking to him until he's sitting quietly (all of him—in all probability—except for his tail), then proceed quietly with the lesson, giving him modulated rewards.

13. If you have more than one dog, don't train the more resilient dog within hearing or sight of the more sensitive one—and don't compare them!

14. Keep your lessons short, brisk and interesting. A dog can't concentrate for long spells. When you start training your dog, train him for 5–10 minutes and, when he's more advanced, 15–20 minutes.

15. The attitudes you display towards an excitable dog should be: (*a*) one of authority and firmness, and (*b*) one of warmth and intimacy. Attitudes of despair, anger, frustration and impatience are neither, and excite or confuse a dog. It's inevitable that you will become frustrated and angry at times, but try to *command* your dog rather than shout at him. Show authority over him rather than anger.

Losing your temper with him can have one of two effects on him. If you're having trouble because you're not displaying enough authority over him, he'll benefit—sometimes the only adequate correction a dog ever gets is in temper! On the other hand, if you're having problems because you're tense, impatient and expecting too much of your dog, losing your temper will impair his training

for the rest of his life. He may never regain complete confidence in you again.

However stupid or unreasonable your dog appears to be, *never blame him*. *You* know what you intend him to do—he can only see what you teach him, and no more. Make allowances for the fact that you have a superior mentality.

16. Aim at controlling your dog with your voice and not with your hands. When you pull a dog toward you, *he* pulls in the opposite direction. And a dog soon learns to dodge grabbing hands!

Also, a dog that's always controlled forcibly is sure to take advantage of his freedom when he gets it. So, remind yourself—use your voice to command, not your hands to grab.

17. Never set yourself a target before a lesson. If you're determined to reach a certain goal before you terminate a session, you're bound to be frustrated on occasions. If, however, after fifteen minutes of training,

your dog doesn't appear to have grasped what you're trying to teach him, there's always a possibility that he'll know the exercise correctly when you start the next lesson.

18. Believe in yourself and reflect this self-confidence. If you *hope* your dog will obey, he won't.

19. The intimate relationship that develops between dog and owner during training should be maintained between lessons. A dog that undergoes training comes to need his master more than he did before.

20. Be in no hurry whatsoever to complete your training programme. Go at your dog's pace. Refer to your instructions frequently (except during lessons), and read them after *each* session to throw light on any mistakes you may be making.

21. If you're struggling with a particular exercise and seem to be making no progress with it, leave it over and work on something your dog enjoys, returning to the sticky exercise some days later when you can both tackle it with a fresh approach. Some dogs even cotton on to an exercise when they see another dog perform it correctly a few times. More than once· I've seen a dog go into the down position after seeing another dog do it, before he's even been commanded—let alone taught!

22. Be *both* patient with your dog's shortcomings *and* deeply appreciative of every effort he makes to please you. He gives up chasing cats and smells and pals; he concentrates hard to avoid corrections, and earn his praise; and he struggles with your mistakes.

23. Without giving up too easily, recognize your own and your dog's limitations. Some people simply don't have the alertness of mind required for the accurate timing that's needed when training a dog, or the range in tone of voice that's required; and some dogs can achieve a higher standard of obedience than others. By

recognizing your own and your dog's limitations, you'll find it easier to be patient with him.

24. Whenever your dog loses confidence, don't continue with his training until you have won his confidence back completely. He may shiver, dribble, repeatedly try to escape with tail and head down, draw away from you, keep offering you a paw, jump up clinging, or look just plain worried. Another symptom of anxiety in a dog is hooking a lip on his tooth, usually coupled with a worried expression on his face. To regain his confidence . . . pause, relax and, if he's a small dog, crouch down; if he is bigger, straddle him. Bend over him so that your face is near his. Speak to him in relaxed and low tones to soothe him and win his trust—as you would soothe a frightened child. Pet him firmly with both hands.

. . . loses confidence . . .

Be in no hurry to continue with the lesson. When you can feel that your dog is no longer holding his head stiff, he's relaxed and confident enough to continue. Continue at a slower pace, with lighter (if any) corrections, warmer rewards, and easier lessons. Command him lightly, and show him less authority. Keep relaxed. If your dog loses confidence too frequently, refer to your instructions to see where you're going wrong.

25. After each training session say 'play-time', have a quick romp with him, give him a drink of water, and—very important—leave him to rest and let the lesson sink in.

26. Between lessons, and when your dog is trained, don't command him too often. When you're out on a walk, for example, let him enjoy his freedom, only commanding him when you have to. Then, not only will your commands have more impact, but he'll obey you more willingly.

Your dog must never be made to feel that obedience is too high a price to pay for giving up his independence.

Conclusion

Just because you know that you can depend on your dog is no reason for making excessive demands on him and subjecting him to unnecessary anxiety.

Many instructions and rules on training and handling your dog may be inconvenient, or incongruous. But you are being taught what is correct, and what is correct is not always convenient or obvious.

However well trained or clever a dog is, he is not a well-programmed automaton but a dog with a personality. He'll still get excited to welcome you home, may get up to a few pranks or take a few chances, still need exercise and affection, still bring in mud and shed hair—but isn't he worth it?

CHAPTER 10

COME ON COMMAND

When a dog ignores a command to come when he's called, his owner probably gives up after a few tries, exasperated with his stubborn and disobedient dog. The dog, meanwhile, is sniffing around watching him out of the corner of his eye to see if he really intends to enforce his command. A little more display of authority, and he'd have jumped to it!

On the other hand, however, there are those that expect push-button responses from their dogs. They expect them to skid instantly to a standstill on a command, ten seconds after being joyfully released on to the inviting

open spaces of a beach. Dogs that reach such a high standard of obedience, such as police and army dogs, are hand-picked, carefully raised and trained and handled by experts—hardly fair competition for the average pet in the home!

To teach your dog to reach the maximum standard of obedience, both that you are able to teach and elicit from him, *and* that he is capable of learning, follow the exercises laid out below. This way you can get him under control when he's within reach, and then gradually achieve the standard where the habit of obedience and joy in receiving praise develop his capacity to obey you from greater distances.

Rules

(*a*) Never command or call your dog when you're not in a position to enforce your command. If you do, he learns one lesson—and that is that you don't have to be taken seriously. If you don't feel like getting up, or your dog's too far away—don't command him. (If you need him urgently, the section on teaching a pup to come when he's called has a few tips on how to get him.)

(*b*) Never call him so often that he finds he has to sacrifice too much to be obedient. He is still a dog with instincts and basic needs to run and sniff and meet other dogs—don't bend him too far.

(*c*) Always make it worth his while to obey by giving him a reward he enjoys.

To teach your dog to come on command, refer to chapter 12 for teaching a dog to walk to heel. This will bring him under control to a certain extent. To develop his will-power, and enable you to bring him under control under more difficult conditions, arrange a distraction for him to work against. This can be, for example, an open car door or another member of your family.

(1) Walk past this distraction, about 6 metres from it. Repeat the procedure you followed when teaching him to walk to heel (commanding, correcting, rewarding and restoring trust), as he tries to dart towards it. Your correction may need to be intensified and, as he resists the temptation to run from you, your reward must be much more exciting.

(2) Over the next few days or weeks, walk a little closer to the distraction, increasing the intensity of your rewards. The closer you get, the more difficult it will become for your dog. (And you!)

Don't make it too difficult for your dog, and don't try to perfect the exercise. You are only developing his will-power and showing him how nice it is to be good! If you cannot achieve the accurate timing required for the exercise, don't continue with it.

To punish your dog for not coming on command *between* training sessions, arm yourself with a stick, a slipper or a clod of grass (depending on his size, his temperament and the thickness of his coat). Stand near enough to aim, and then command him. Should he obey you, follow the usual routine of restoring trust and rewarding him—but should he ignore you, throw! Don't worry about injuring him, you won't. When hit, he should be put out enough to be considerably startled—but not enough to make him run away in terror.

You must offer him refuge and restore trust immediately, rewarding him profusely when he does come. If he runs away, however, but simply so that he can be out of range to continue his sniffing about in peace, you have a resilient dog and may never get him under control! If he just strolls over to investigate what it was that hit him, you didn't hit him hard enough.

If, however, you *miss* your dog, don't throw again. You may end up losing your temper, and he'll regard dodging the slipper as a sport. If you managed to startle him—restore trust. If you crouch *right down*, you'll double your chances of getting him to come to you—and better luck next time! (Should you find when you restore trust that your dog just looks at you and tells you where you can get off to, you're probably under-correcting him. Or perhaps your tone of voice is lacking warmth, and you just don't convince him. Correct him adequately, restore trust very warmly, and give him *very* spirited praise.)

The next time you command your dog, he should look up quickly in anticipation of the missile, not at all eager to repeat the experience, whereupon you crouch down immediately and praise him. He will be relieved not to be under attack again—and will, of course, get his due reward for coming.

If your aim is poor, a clod scatters and may do the trick! If your timing is slow, command and throw together.

Something else you can do to teach your dog to come when he's called is to let him drag a rope, about 6 metres long, when you're out on a walk. As he runs past you, command him 'Heel!' and, instead of throwing a slipper at him, step on the rope. This will jerk him to an immediate stop. Then restore trust to bring him to you, and reward him when he comes. (This will be more effective on sand, cement, or gravel, than on grass, where the rope won't grip as well.)

If it keeps sliding out, put a knot in it.

Just watch out, though, that he doesn't run around you and then off. If you don't do a quick jump, you'll see stars—day or night!

When your dog is *very* distracted, command him 'Jason, heel!' Your voice must be crisp—not loud, and

208

must ring with authority. If you shout at him, it doesn't have the same impact. A good tip if you really need your command to carry is to say 'Hey!' instead of 'Heel!' at the same time making a noise by scraping or stamping your foot, or clapping.

If your dog is only mildly distracted when you want to call him, say 'Jason, come boy!' brightly. But if he's all ears when you want him to come to you, your *reward* is your command. Pat your side and say 'Good boy, Jason!' warmly, and he'll be right with you. Save your commands with impact for when you really need them.

At all times, keep your sessions short, enjoyable and not too difficult—a little work correctly done goes a long way—and don't command your dog too often. Let him enjoy his running, so that coming to you never becomes tedious.

When your dog reaches such a high standard of obedience that he begins to actually anticipate a command and he obeys it before you give it, *do* reward him. If, for instance, he sees the milkman, is about to rush out and take a chunk out of his leg, but looks at you and thinks better of it, reward him *as if* he had obeyed a command, or his high standard of obedience will start slipping.

Allow time, the habit of obedience, correct handling, repetition and plenty of pleasurable rewards over the weeks and months, to develop your dog's full potential for coming on command.

CHAPTER 11

SIT AND STAY

A. Sit

Teaching a dog to sit isn't always as easy as you'd expect, because some dogs, when told to sit, stiffen. Never refuse to continue with your training programme just because your dog is not yet sitting on command. Allow this to right itself as the dog becomes less tense and more eager to please you.

1. Put your check chain on your dog as described in chapter 9.
2. Holding the lead short in your right hand, stand close to him on his right side.
3. Pet him a little.
4. Put your left hand on the base of his spine. If he tries to dodge out sideways use this hand to hold him against you.
5. Draw the lead up and back, pushing him down with your left hand. If necessary, use your right knee against his chest to push him back gently. While you're doing this:
6. Say firmly: 'Jason, sit!' Because you are pushing him back and holding him firmly, he should sit automatically.
7. Reward him very warmly, as if he'd sat of his own accord! Forget about the fact that he didn't earn it — make him eager to repeat it.
8. Let him run around a little before you repeat this.

After a few times, if he doesn't oblige on the 'sit' command, instead of pushing him down, smack him lightly.

Repeat 1–8 a few times.

If, however, when you command your dog to sit, he stiffens his back legs in resistance, or bucks around, handle him this way:

Follow 1, 2 and 3 above. Then:

4. Hold the lead half-way down in your *left* hand.
5. Say 'Jason, sit!', and simultaneously—
6. Either: with your right hand, bring the loose end of the lead over on to his hindquarters sharply to sting him; or: give the check chain a sharp jerk.
7. Reward him extra warmly. If this is done correctly, he should tuck his hindquarters in instantly on the impact, thus sitting automatically.
8. Reward him extra warmly.

Don't resort to this sharp correction if your dog is apprehensive or anxious or during the early stages of training. Simply push him into the sitting position. Resort to sharper measures when he has more confidence, and he's obviously just being stubborn.

If, instead of sitting properly, he merely bends his legs slightly in response, a light 'Good dog!' should make him go all the way down.

If your dog still stiffens on the sit command when he knows perfectly well what's expected of him, a good tip to make him relax, and therefore sit, is to say firmly but kindly, 'Sit, boy'.

If, when your dog sits, he leans against you, step away suddenly. When he finds he can no longer depend on your legs to support him, he'll support himself.

If he drops on to his belly when you command him, you are probably being too hard on him. At least he's trying. Let the clasp rest against the opposite side of your dog's neck so that the lead is under his chin and supports him when you command him. Reward him warmly immediately he sits. If the reward makes him flop down again, reward him warmly *and* lightly without bending over him.

If he flops on to one side or sits on the base of his spine like a baboon, put him straight. With a little luck, if you put him straight often enough—he'll start sitting straight himself! It takes patience because he's not aware of the way he is sitting. A dog that flops over may be a bit young for training, or he may be bored. More brisk, interesting lessons should help correct this.

Don't give the 'sit' command too often, or your dog will get bored with it.

B. Sit from Down Position

When you teach your dog to sit up from the down position, stand next to him, pat your side, and say invitingly and lightly, 'Sit, boy!', then pat the head that pops up and noses between your thigh and hand. If he hesitates, a warm reward may prompt him to sit up for a pat. You don't command with authority in this exercise, and if you're tense, he *won't* sit up.

C. Stay

Some dogs, when told to stay, are glad of a snooze— or, as Kinney puts it: 'do so in a distracted, absent-minded, like-eating-peanuts-sort-of-a-way.' Others hate staying still, and there are those that cannot bear the separation. They really think their owner is going away for ever!

212

To teach this last type of dog to stay in one place for any length of time:

1. Put the lead on him.
2. Get him into sitting position.
3. Stand in front of him, right up close to him, holding his chin in your left hand so that he looks up at your face. But don't bend right down over him, or he'll probably jump up into your face. Hold the loop of the lead in your right hand.
4. Be completely relaxed.
5. If your dog is over-excited, soothe him as described in chapter 9, point 12.
6. Don't move away from him, just say 'Stay!' very sharply, keeping quite relaxed and *still petting him lovingly.*
7. Wait half a second.
8. Release him (see below). He's done absolutely nothing to earn this reward, but that doesn't matter!

Pat him and praise him as if he's just done something quite outstanding!

9. Allow him to let off steam for a while.

10. Repeat this several times, until you no longer startle him when you say 'Stay!' sharply—because he is so busy anticipating his reward!

11. After he's let off steam, repeat points 1–4 above. Pet him lovingly, and while you're doing this move your feet *one* pace back. He shouldn't notice this.

12. Say 'Jason, stay!'.

13. Maintaining a hard attitude, stand up abruptly.

14. Standing upright, wait for only half a second, keeping your finger pointed, and assuming a very formidable expression and attitude to *hold* him from you.

15. Release him.
16. Repeat this several times.
17. After he's bounced about in an excited manner for a few seconds, stimulated by your praise, calm him (point 12 in chapter 9) completely, standing close to him and petting him *firmly* with two hands, and speaking to him soothingly.
18. *While* you're petting him switch off and say 'Jason, stay!'
19. Then step away abruptly with a harsh facial expression, upright bearing and pointed finger, which should hold him from you.
20. Release him after a second—only a second, no more. You literally switch from a soft attitude to a hard one and back to a soft attitude in a few seconds.
21. Without straining your dog, increase slowly at his pace, from one pace and one second, to two paces and two seconds, and so on.

You've been aiming at showing your dog that you *are* coming back after all, and that to stay is not such a terrible thing as he thought it was—it actually earns him exciting praise!

If, however, your dog is not 'clingy', short-cut the parts that aren't necessary for him, working at his pace.

If he doesn't even *want* to get up and come to you when you release him ('like-eating-peanuts-sort-of-a-way'), use a turf clod to budge him as described for come on command, and restore trust so that he doesn't run away. It works like a charm, and once he's been budged, he may even enjoy his lesson!

While you're following the above procedure, adhere strictly to these rules:

1. Always be sure that your dog is not tense and anxious

before your 'stay' command. A dog needing reassurance will fight through any punishment to remain close to his owner.

2. Don't say 'Stay!' until your dog is actually sitting.

3. Move away in an upright position. It's a common mistake to bend over a dog after giving the 'Stay!' command. This usually makes a dog creep forward instead of staying.

4. Always give the 'Stay!' command with the *end* of the lead in your hand. Don't find it after you've said 'Stay!', or slide your hand down the lead as you move away—you may have difficulty making your dog stay with such distractions.

5. Make sure that:

   (a) your *reassuring* attitude before you give the stay command,

   (b) your *hard* attitude when you command your dog to stay and then move away, and

   (c) the *pleasure* you show when you release your dog,

   are all distinct—they must not overlap in any way. Switch from one to the other abruptly. An anxious dog can just about break down with anxiety without this clarity.

6. Be very strict with the stay exercise. You were lenient with the sit exercise, but now you should display the utmost authority. Stern facial expression, upright bearing, firm voice and finger pointed as a signal after your stay command, all *help* your dog to stay.

7. While your dog is learning to stay, keep your finger pointed as a signal on every stay exercise.

8. Always be completely confident that he *will* stay. Uncertainty will draw him to you. Use your eyes to hold your dog from you. A stern and confident look in your eyes will help hold him.

216

9. *Never linger in front of your dog after your 'Stay!' command to see if he is going to stay!* Once you've said 'Stay!', *go!*, whether it's simply into an upright position, when you start teaching the exercise, or a few paces back, at a more advanced stage. If you hesitate to see if he's going to stay, *he won't!* He'll either find this proximity unnerving or he'll think you're releasing him. This is the most common mistake beginners make when teaching their dogs to stay.

10. Teach your dog with very short 'Stays!' that you are *coming back* before you actually teach him that he must stay.

11. Make the release great fun.

12. Never walk back slowly after you've told your dog to stay. Walk briskly.

13. Keep this exercise a little easier than your dog can actually manage. If you say 'Stay!', and then go out of sight, when he's only been taught to stay for a few paces, you'll make the task of teaching him to stay much more difficult for yourself and him.

14. Never praise your dog for staying or show any pleasure whatsoever in his staying until he's released. (When he is fully trained, of course, it won't matter so much.)

15. Distractions, such as talking to someone else (until he's been specifically taught to stay under such circumstances); stumbling while moving from him, and so on, will all be false alarms to him, and he'll come bounding up to you, thinking he's been released.

16. At the beginning of the next lesson, never start where you left off on the last one. If, at the end of your last lesson for instance, you were teaching your dog to stay 10 paces, don't begin your next lesson with this distance. Begin your next lesson moving a short distance away (and praising him as if it were 10 paces!) and then quickly work up to where you left off last time. Then gradually continue to improve his stay distance.

17. Don't expect your dog to learn to stay near his kennel, another person, the front door, etc. You'll get furious when he keeps running there for refuge during the lesson if it gets a little difficult for him!

18. *Never* see how far you can get. By doing this, you'll be encouraging your dog to be disobedient.

19. Never release him *because* you see him coming—correct him. (See below for correcting a dog when he gets up before he's been released.)

20. Stop the lesson *before* he starts feeling strained.

21. Let the progress your dog makes dictate the speed with which you increase the distance he stays. Don't set yourself a target before you start the lesson—it's bound to lead to frustration on occasions.

22. When you are leaving your dog for some time, don't give him the 'stay' command. He must know the difference between on and off duty. If he *does* get up, you won't be there to correct him.

D. Release (Recall)

To release your dog from the 'sit and stay' position, put out your arms in a welcoming gesture, bend over, say 'That's a clever dog!', 'Good boy!' or 'There's a good dog!', which make him come bouncing up to you with joy. 'Come' or 'Heel' or indifferent praise won't give you such a keen and interested pupil as will extravagant praise conveying pride and pleasure. If he comes

too slowly, stimulate him, pat your thighs, run from him
—make a game of it until he's speeded up his recall.

When you release your dog, don't release him at the
same instant as you stop moving away from him, or
he'll start coming to you *because* you stop. Hold him
with your stern aspect and finger-signal for varying
periods (1–10 seconds), then release him.

E. Corrections for Sit and Stay

You cannot convey confidence to your dog while you
are teaching him to sit and stay if you don't know what
to do if he gets up before you release him. When you
correct him, it will be either for:

(1) trying to come to you prematurely, or
(2) trying to escape the lesson.

(a) When do you correct him?

You correct your dog the very instant his head goes
down to lever up his hindquarters. If you wait to see if
perhaps he will change his mind, he won't! If you hesitate,
in no time he's in full gallop and by then it's too late to
stop him.

(b) How do you correct him?

(i) *If your dog is still on the lead*

(1) Repeat your 'stay' command, and simultaneously —
(2) step forward to
(3) string him up as sharply as his temperament will
     permit. This correction must be worth avoiding —
     but no more;
(4) holding him up, say 'Stay!' again sharply;
(5) loosen your hold on the lead (whether you move
     back or not here depends on how advanced your
     lessons are);

(6)   standing upright, with a stern expression, keep your finger pointed for just a second;

(7)   release him abruptly and warmly.

(ii) *If your dog is not on the lead*

Adjust the correction that suits him. This may be an intimidating step towards him; a sharp verbal correction as demonstrated; a shaking; or nothing short of a fist in the face. If, however, you have a very willing dog, just take him back to the place where you told him to stay. Whichever you do, repeat the stay command.

(1)   Step forward instantly, and say 'stay';

(2)   correct him (as described—a step, a verbal correction, a shaking, etc.);

(3)   step back instantly whatever you do! *Don't* linger to see if he intends to heed you;

(4)   keep your finger pointed;

(5)   keep the length of time he stays after the correction *short*;

(6)   release him warmly.

If your correction startled your dog and he is upset, crouch down to his level when you release him. If you over-correct him and he turns tail, restore trust instantly to get him back. Don't step towards him or try to go after him. Use only your voice to win his confidence and get him back. If he's too afraid to come back, go to him (probably in his kennel), reassure him, bring him back calmly to the lesson and terminate it with a couple of easy exercises, giving him ample praise. Make your corrections lighter in future.

If your dog always sits promptly whenever he's verbally corrected, but still needs *repeated* corrections, walk decisively up to him and punish him physically—in spite of the fact that he obeyed your verbal correction. He's a chancer!

An effective correction for a repeated offender is a good shaking.

Your dog's eyes betray his scheming mind. If he keeps looking left and right (usually with his head held slightly down) but still stays, he's reluctant to stay. But with repetition, easy lessons and plenty of rewards, he should learn to stay willingly. Instead of trying to plan an escape, he'll start to wait eagerly for his rewards. (If they're worth waiting for!) If your dog won't hold your eye, keep your lessons short, easy and fun, until he does.

It takes a little practice to adjust the correction that holds your dog from you, yet keeps him from running away in fright.

After a correction, always step back immediately. If you hang around in front of him to see if he has taken note of your correction, he *will* creep up to you.

Never reward a dog for taking heed of a correction until after he has been released.

One common mistake beginners make when they correct their dogs in the sit and stay exercise is this: instead of correcting their dog, they keep stepping back, hoping he'll change his mind. The dog doesn't and keeps stepping forward. By the time he's reached his owner, his owner has lost all hope that he'll change his mind, and realizing now that he *has* to use physical correction after all, thumps the dog's backside. The dog, gleefully wagging his tail, loves every moment of it, and the poor despairing owner gives up!

(c) **Why does a dog refuse to stay despite repeated corrections?**

If, in spite of repeated corrections, your dog keeps coming to you before you release him:

(1) Your correction may be too mild;

(2) your command may not be clear or forceful enough;

(3) you may be forgetting the finger signal;

(4) you may be hesitating before you move back after your stay command;

(5) you may be walking back too slowly after your stay command;

(6) you may be expecting your dog to stay too long;

(7) your lessons may be too long;

(8) you may be bending over him when you move back;

(9) you may be displaying too little authority;

(10) your dog may be too smart.

If your dog tries to escape his lesson (*not* because you are making the lessons too difficult or frightening him, but because he is genuinely naughty) the section on 'heeling free' in chapter 12 will advise you on how to get him back. However, to cure him, follow the procedure laid out below:

1. Tie a rope securely on to the end of your dog's lead. The rope should be about 6 metres long.

2. Either stretch the rope out in front of you so that you can step on to it, to prevent your dog from getting away, or tie it to a post. (If you tie it to a post, be very careful, especially if he's a big dog. If he runs around you and then off, you can come quite a cropper if you don't do a quick sideways jump. The rope shouldn't be too long if its tied to a post. Your dog may just injure himself if he is brought up *too* sharply while running away at top speed.)

3. Continue with your sit and stay exercises,
   (*a*) making your rewards excessive;
   (*b*) keeping the lessons very easy; and
   (*c*) crouching down when you release him.

This all means that you're, firstly, diminishing your dog's reasons for wanting to escape the lesson and, secondly, increasing his reason for wanting to work with you. If the only escape from correction is to be obedient, and, if that itself is easy and pleasurable, he must, in time, learn to stay.

When your dog runs off in the middle of his lesson, he'll be pulled up sharply at the end of his rope. This *should* be sufficient punishment for him. You must therefore restore trust so that *he* comes to *you* (not *you* to *him*). Reward him *profusely* as if he had *made* the decision to be obedient and not as if he had had no choice. Repeat. Keep it *easy* and *fun*, so that he *wants* to obey.

If getting trapped at the end of the cord is not sufficient punishment for him, you have a resilient dog with a high threshold of correction. This type of dog should preferably be trained by an expert.

Some dogs are very shrewd and know perfectly well that they are fastened and therefore don't try to escape unless they are free. This dog might be fooled if a second check chain is fastened to the rope and, after this is placed on him, a great show is made of throwing the lead away. Such a dog might then think he's free. However, a clever dog like this is very difficult to train.

After a great deal of repetition, when your dog finds the lessons are, after all, great fun, and the habit of obedience is firmly establishing itself in his behaviour, the cord can be abandoned.

When the cord is off, he doesn't *have* to stay any more. If he does, it's because he *wants* to. So *make* him want to. Make your rewards excessive. Crouch down when you release him. Keep the length of your 'Stays!' very short, gradually working up to the length of time you had taught him to stay while fastened to the cord.

If, however, your dog is dismissing himself from the lesson because he's anxious, all you do to get him back is to crouch down and say 'All right, boy, good dog!' lovingly and warmly. *Do not step towards him.* If you're quite relaxed and handle the situation correctly, your dog will come back immediately. Reassure him completely when he comes (as described in chapter 9, point 24). Make his corrections lighter, his rewards warmer, his lessons easier, and be more relaxed when you train him.

When your dog is staying for quite a few paces, start walking around him—but don't go behind him until he's quite confident. Give him *extra* praise when he resists the urge to turn himself around (but he can, of course, turn his head to watch you). Keep your finger pointed and with a stern expression on your face all the time while you walk around him—watching him closely all the time and correcting him the instant he needs correction—but *don't* strain him.

When you see that your dog's staying quite happily, without any signs of anxiety, you can start turning your back on him.

Half turn for a couple of exercises, watching him over your shoulder. Then take your eyes off him for one or two paces. Increase this gradually. There are various ways you can keep a check on him. You can keep his shadow in view, so that, when he thinks you're not watching, he's caught cheating 'red-handed'. A third

person can signal you when a correction is needed, or you can watch his reflection in a window.

When you turn and face him again, don't release him immediately, otherwise he'll start coming *because* you turn. Stop. Turn. Stand with your finger pointed as a signal, for varying periods, then release him.

A rather amusing situation can develop when a dog isn't being handled firmly enough. His owner walks away, with the dog creeping after him. The owner glances over his shoulder, the dog sits immediately. Satisfied, the owner walks a few more paces with, unknown to him, his dog shadowing him again. He turns, and the dog sits—you can almost see his halo glowing! The poor owner can't understand how his dog came to be so far from where he was left sitting—and never gets to train his clever dog to perfection! This happens, of course, when there's not enough authority, and the punishments are too light. However, although such a dog can be exasperating to train, he's usually fun to own!

F. Out of Sight

Your dog is ready to learn to be left in the 'sit' position while you go out of sight, when you can walk about 10 metres from him without his showing any sign of anxiety.

1. Place him in a position about 10 metres from a corner.
2. Say 'stay!' firmly.
3. Walk to the corner.
4. Turn and face him, showing a prominent forefinger.
5. Repeat 'Stay!'
6. Slip out of sight for one second, preferably leaving a hand or foot in view.
7. Reappear.
8. Repeat 'Stay!'

226

9. Let him wait one second.
10. Release him.

Repeat this, slowly increasing the time you remain out of sight. You are showing him that you are *coming back* before you actually teach him to wait for your return. (It's only for the first couple of exercises that you need leave a hand or a foot in view.)

When you reach the stage that you are out of sight for some time, only do it from where you can still keep an eye on him (through a window for instance), should you need to correct him. Correct him immediately, or it won't be as effective.

The slower you increase the amount of time you remain out of sight, the less strain your lessons, the warmer your rewards — the longer he will ultimately stay.

If you see a head popping around the corner to find you while you are 'hiding', anything less than a sharp correction will be interpreted as encouragement, so pleased will he be with himself at finding you.

Once you have taught your dog to stay, make it clear to him when is 'on' and 'off' duty. It's hardly fair to him to tell him to 'Stay!', then go out of sight, find a friend, and chat a couple of hours, while your dog is in a dilemma about whether he's allowed to run around or not!

I don't personally like leaving dogs for long stretches. Some clubs do, and this does subject their dogs to considerable anxiety.

When you leave your dog in the 'stay' position for any length of time, tell him to lie down first, so that he doesn't have to stay sitting up in a tiring position.

CHAPTER 12

HEELWORK

Place the check chain and lead on your dog as indicated in chapter 9. Place him on your left-hand side with the lead in your right hand, holding it both half-way down and at the loop end. This way, it's not so long that you trip over it, and when your dog moves away from you, you can drop the first-mentioned part of the lead without it tightening. (For dogs that won't work properly on the lead, see p. 292.)

Your left hand is free to jerk the check chain when necessary, and for petting, encouraging and praising your dog.

(1) As you move forward, say pleasantly and lightly 'Heel, boy!' or 'Jason, heel!', depending on whether you have his full attention, or whether his mind is on other matters. *Note:* say 'heel' *as* you go, not *after* you've gone!

(2) Walk around with him for a few minutes (or, if necessary, for a few lessons), going where *he* wants to go. Talk to him and pet him, passing the lead from hand to hand as he goes from your right- to your left-hand side. Do this for a while until he enjoys the experience of walking with you.

(3) Now start the serious work, and set yourself a straight path, aiming for an object, like a tree or a pole, some distance away. Watch him closely so that you can anticipate his movements. (To teach your dog to *stay* at your left side, see below.)

In fact, you should watch your dog so closely that you'll have to check beforehand that there are no pot-holes, flower-beds or trees—because, while watching your dog so closely, you would walk right into them!

(4) When your dog runs ahead of you, here's the crunch: let the lead slacken.

You're going to find this very difficult, because it goes against all your natural reactions when trying to control a dog; but learning to drive a car is also just as confusing in the beginning! As you slacken the lead—give the command 'Jason, heel!' as demonstrated. In order to keep the lead slack, you may have to step toward him. If you simply heave your dog back on to the path, you've achieved no more than getting him back where you wanted him for the moment. And if you command *and* jerk together you are, in fact, commanding and punishing simultaneously—and that's hardly fair, is it?

(5) In a split second you must discern whether or not he's stopping in obedience to your 'heel' command.

(a) If he stops, step back a pace and reward him that very instant to show he has done right. But, whatever you do, you must not touch him or take one step towards him. Pat him only when *he* comes all the way up to you himself. Your reward should bring him to you. If he doesn't come *right* up close to you, step away from him again and repeat 'That's a good dog!' warmly, patting your side. When he comes right up to your side, give him all the patting he has then deserved, and reward him as demonstrated, continuing with the heel exercise.

(b) But, should he ignore your 'heel' command (which is more likely), give the check chain a jerk (don't pull him—jerk the chain sharply upwards so that it tightens, then loosens immediately). How sharply you jerk depends on how sensitive or stubborn your dog is. He should be startled—but not terrified, whereupon you step back a pace and restore trust. Again, you only pet him when he comes *all* the way up to you, and only crouch down *if necessary* when you restore trust—or you're sure to land flat on your back! Reward him profusely when he comes to you.

Your dog is more likely to come three or four paces to you than only a short distance of about one pace. This is why you should step away from him when you restore trust.

However, if you can't achieve close work by your voice alone, hold your lead a little tighter—but only so that it tightens if your dog steps *out* of line.

To teach your dog to stay at your left side during the heel exercise, handle him as follows:

230

When he comes to the wrong side, stop. Step over him so that he's on your left, hug him, praise him profusely and continue.

If, after several lessons, he doesn't take the hint, handle him thus:

(1) When he comes around to your right, *stop*.

(2) Command him 'Heel!'

(3) Reprimand him or smack his nose with your right hand.

(4) Turn your body around (so that he can follow the direction of your voice).

(5) And, patting your left side, swivel slightly to make your left side more accessible to him.

(6) Restore trust over your left shoulder, rewarding him as he comes.

(7) Praise him warmly and pat him when he's at your left side.

(8) Continue with the exercise.

If he keeps hesitating just behind you, simply crouch down, and he'll come straight around into position. Reward him, get up and continue walking.

Although you are actually saying 'Good dog!', don't touch him until he's *at* your left side. This is because it may prevent him from coming all the way around. As long as he's being petted just behind you, why should he make that extra effort? But when he does come around to be patted, *pet him very warmly*; in fact you can even throw your arms around his neck!

Note

(a) Neither your 'heel' command nor your correction makes him come around to your left side.

(b) The loving 'Good dog!' coming from behind your back after his fright (from the punishment at your right side) makes him come around.

(c) Don't repeat 'Heel!' after your punishment—restore trust.

(d) When he comes around to your left side, let him think he's very clever.

(e) Don't withhold 'Good dog!' after you correct him just because you don't feel he's deserved it yet. Use it to *bring* him there.

(f) *Repeat:* don't pet him until he's come *all* the way around. If he's so anxious that he needs a touch to reassure him, touch him and say 'Good dog!' then withdraw your hand. Keep relaxed. If necessary simply crouch down, and reward him warmly when this brings him around on to your lap.

All this is very similar to chapter 13, 'Coming to the left side', and both can be mastered together.

When your dog comes around to your right-hand side during heelwork, always stop before you correct him. Don't correct him while you're walking.

A. Right-angle turns

Practise 90° turns before you attempt right-about turns. Because your dog looks up to his right to look at you, turn right more often to keep him concentrating.

To teach your dog right-angle turns, follow the directions given for right-about turns, but do only a 90° and not a 180° turn.

Whether you're doing right, left, right-about or left-about turns, practise *without* your dog if you can't keep your balance or if you can't manage your footwork. (Just make sure your neighbours are not watching!)

B. Right-about turns

If you're heeling along happily and suddenly do a right-about turn, your dog will probably go straight on because he's not a mind-reader.

To do this correctly

(a) step on to your right foot;
(b) pat your left side;
(c) say 'Jason, heel!'

all simultaneously.

Then swivel, and to keep him close—*praise him* as he turns with you. Then walk back along the same path (i.e. not doing an untidy U-turn). He'll probably walk wide or straight on, hesitate or short-cut behind you.

(i) If he walks wide or straight on because he's not concentrating, say 'Jason, heel!' and give the check chain a quick upward flick and restore trust immediately. Reward him warmly when he comes close and continue with your corner. When he turns close corners after this, because he doesn't want to be punished, give him extra praise. (*That's* a clever boy!) Be careful not to overpunish, or he'll hesitate when turning a corner, in anticipation of a correction.

(ii) If he walks wide or straight on because he's bored, or your directions are not clear, your commands too soft or your timing wrong, correct this—not him.

Some people, when their dog keeps on turning wide corners, try working at the end of a passage. The dog *has* to stay close, finds it's *nice* to be close and, after a lot of practice, *stays* close when returned to normal training conditions.

(iii) If he hesitates or walks wide because he's anxious, say 'Good boy!' warmly to dispel his anxiety and to 'draw' him close. You must, however, keep relaxed or he won't come close to you.

(iv) If he keeps short-cutting, stop before your corner, give him a heel command and turn slowly *with* him, rewarding him all the way. Increase the speed of your turns gradually. If necessary, you may have to master 'Coming to the left side' before you can turn your corners properly.

Give a heel command before *each* corner, and *praise* him each time he turns a corner. There is, of course, no need to say you don't drag your dog around, especially when he is hesitating anxiously.

C. Left-about turns

For the inexperienced handler, this is a more difficult exercise. Rather than confuse your dog, attempt to teach him only when you're making good progress with your lessons.

(*a*) Step on to your left foot;
(*b*) do a *complete* left-about turn without your dog;
(*c*) pass the lead behind your back as you turn; say 'Good boy!' over your left shoulder;
(*d*) pat your left side and say 'Heel, boy!'

When you pat your side, and say 'Good boy!' over your left shoulder, he should recover your side again, happy to see that after losing you for an instant all is well again.

You may have to master 'Coming to the left side' first if you struggle with this, but it's actually easier than it sounds!

Heelwork is not a Sunday afternoon stroll, nor is it a military exercise. It's work for you, and fun for your dog. Walk up, down, turning right and left, doing right-and left-about turns, figures of eight, praising and patting him—and, as he becomes more experienced, make the turns more frequent.

Continue walking your dog to heel, commanding and correcting him when necessary, as described above, and rewarding him while he's walking at your side. Praise him as his temperament requires; and work with your lead *slack* all the time, except when it tightens for a correction.

If your dog refuses to come to you after you command or correct him, be careful to assess accurately whether it's because he's confused and anxious or because he needs a stronger correction.

When your dog begins to stay close to you to avoid being punished, praise him profusely and pat him constantly, making it nice for him to walk beside you.

Once again, do not pet your dog when you say 'Good dog!' after a command or a correction, until he has come *right* up to you, encouraged by the warmth in your voice, otherwise he'll see no reason for making that extra effort. When he comes *all* the way up to you, *then* you pat him all he deserves! (And more!)

If your dog keeps on running ahead of you, in spite of repeated corrections, both correct him more severely *and* turn and walk in the opposite direction after your correction. Pat your side, say 'Heel!' and give him extra praise when he comes.

If he's a tough dog, and you're not strong enough to jerk the check chain adequately, hold the lead in your left hand, and a light stick in your right hand. As he runs

235

ahead, say 'Jason, heel!' He'll ignore you of course, so, keeping the lead slack, aim at his legs with the stick and he'll stop and look around to see what hit him. *Restore trust* very lovingly, crouching down and stepping back if necessary. Praise him profusely when he comes and walk on, praising him warmly as he stays with you—which he'll do if you handled him correctly. Repeat the 'heel' command when he next runs ahead and he should stop dead immediately to make quite sure he's not under attack again. Don't touch him—let him come to you—and reward him as if he's brilliant! Turn and walk in the opposite direction, praising your dog profusely to regain his confidence.

You probably won't have to use the stick again—he should now be adequately punished by his check chain. If he limps for a moment after you used the stick, don't worry; continue your lesson lovingly—you won't injure him. He is, of course, a tough dog, or you wouldn't have had to resort to a stick.

When you jerk the check chain, you must never (or try not to) pull and command simultaneously, because it isn't fair to punish your dog before he has actually disobeyed you. Give him a chance to show you that he *can* obey. Also—you don't want him to say, 'Aha!, I am free to go now!', when he's off the lead and hears the 'heel' command—and feels no tug!

Before going on, we'll make a few suggestions on how you can handle your dog if he has his own ideas about how he thinks a dog should walk on a lead.

1. *If he wanders around*

Your dog isn't concentrating and needs more colourful handling. Handle him with more authority. Make your commands crisper and your punishments sharper. Your rewards must be much more exciting; pat your side and talk to him all the time while he walks in the correct position. And give him a few more unexpected turns to help him keep his mind on his lessons a little more.

2. *If he jumps up against you*

A dog jumps up either because he's too exuberant or because he is needing reassurance.

An exuberant dog jumps up and down repeatedly with a cocky expression, panting happily in his owner's face, and the more he's shouted at, the more he does it. An anxious dog jumps up and tries to cling to his owner.

If your dog is jumping up because he's too boisterous, handle him as described for problem dogs that jump up. Display plenty of authority over him, and modulate

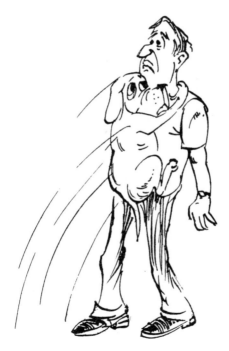

your rewards so as not to stimulate him. But you have a willing worker—and, for that, you're lucky! Don't dampen your dog's spirits, but let the final polish come with time and practice.

If your dog is jumping up because he's anxious, there is something wrong with the way you're handling him. He can't speak, so jumping up and clinging to you is his way of telling you he's unhappy. You're probably expecting too much from him or handling him too harshly. Keep calm; don't shout; command him quietly and firmly and give him ample reassurance—while he has four feet on the ground, not two.

To reassure him, speak to him as demonstrated for reassuring a confused dog in chapter 9 and stand close to him, petting him firmly and lovingly for some time. Don't pet him gently, or he'll jump up again. Use *two* hands, both to pet him with, *and* to hold him down with if he tries to shoot a wet nose into your face. After he's completely reassured, punish any further attempts to jump up.

Keep the lessons short and not too frequent, going at your dog's pace, and not expecting too much from him, but at the same time, handling him *very* firmly. Give him plenty of warm and convincing praise and show deep appreciation for each effort he makes to please you. He'll probably also take quite a heavy punishment, although he tries pretty hard to disguise it!

This reaction is one often seen in a dog that is not temperamentally suited to his owner. The dog needs a more intense owner, and his owner should have a bolder dog to handle.

3. *If he keeps flopping or walking across your feet*

Firstly, instead of going in a clockwise direction as you'll undoubtedly find yourself doing, walk in an *anti-*clockwise circle.

To do this, you'll have to be very firm with your dog.

Once again, he is probably displaying anxiety. As suggested for dogs that jump up, give him both ample reassurance and be very firm with him. When he's completely reassured, correct him for pushing in front of you. Put your left hand on the lead connection near his neck, palm facing back, and each time he moves in front of you say 'Heel!' and give a short, sharp backward jerk. The very *instant* you see him walking correctly, both praise him *and* walk faster. Pet him all the time you are walking and praise him for escaping punishment by clinging to the correct position.

If sharp jerks are not enough to keep him in check, smack the face that noses around in front of you.

Keep the lead tight while he's trying to push in front of you, *praising* him for staying at your side (which you are actually *forcing* him to do) and allow it to remain loose only when he doesn't keep straining on it. Keep petting and praising him both while you hold him back in position and when he stays there voluntarily.

If he's very tense and flops on his tummy across your feet, pull him up into a sitting position, straddle him (to hold him up and prevent him from flopping down again) and reassure him completely—the proximity of your face will help to keep him up. When you've won his confidence completely, you can start working with him again—always walk fast with him, giving him very extravagant praise. Pat your side lightly, a little higher than his head, to encourage him to hold his head up. When he holds his head up, pat it lovingly.

4. *If he walks to heel too slowly*

This is very difficult—and in some dogs, impossible—to correct. Dogs heel slowly because they're nervous and anxious; or placid and lazy; or bored.

If your dog heels slowly because he's anxious, this is probably because you're tense or impatient with him. You correct this easily by reassuring him to 'draw' him up to you.

To regain confidence, you must be patient and relaxed. Pat your side and say 'All right, good boy!' in low and loving tones, warmly and convincingly as demonstrated. He'll be only too pleased to discover that he can trust you enough to stay close to you.

If your dog walks slowly because he is lazy, trot with him, pat your side and talk brightly to him. If you scratch his back in a delicious manner while you're praising him—*only* while he's in the correct position—it may also help him get into the habit of heeling close to you. Praise him extravagantly while he walks alongside you. Stimulating a lazy heeler and making a game of it are the only ways you can cure him. Always walk fast once you've corrected him. Be reassured—you haven't got headaches when it comes to teaching him to sit and stay!

If, however, your dog is heeling slowly because he's bored stiff, make your lessons much more interesting for him.

Yet another reason for a dog walking too slowly is so that he can work out a plan to get free of his lesson. He doesn't like being trained and is probably smart enough to force you to abandon your efforts by making it too difficult for you!

5. *If he walks with his head held right down*

Speak to your dog lightly and cheerfully if he develops this habit, only touching his head if it comes up. Walk quite fast, giving minimum correction and the maximum praise. Don't bend over him, keep upright, patting your side while his head is down, and patting his head when he lifts it up. If you run lightly he may lift his head to enter into the spirit of the fun.

6. *If he plays with the lead*

If your dog keeps playing with his lead, it may be because he's too young for training (see page 95). If he's not too young, however, be very firm with him. Each time he grabs the lead, smack his nose and say 'Leave!', then continue with the lesson. Give him modulated rewards so as not to excite him, and be very authoritative.

If, however, he keeps trying to take the lead out of your hand by hooking his front leg over it, he's probably anxious. Make the lessons easier, your corrections lighter, and your rewards warmer; and then, when he puts his foot on the lead, jerk the lead sharply upwards, which he won't like. Handle him with extremes of firmness and authority and warmth and praise. Always keep relaxed while training him.

7. *If he keeps lying on his back*

If your dog rolls over on to his back with pleading eyes, looking most indecent, suggesting that to have his tummy tickled would be much nicer than to be trained, *do not* give in to him. Step away from him. Hold the lead

by the loop with your right hand, and give it a downward jerk (how sharply you jerk depends on his temperament). Pat your side and say 'Good boy!' warmly, which will get him over his shock at discovering you could ever be so hard-hearted. Then let *him* come to *you*. If he won't, crouch down. Continue with the exercise, giving him ample praise and not too much correction.

(A dog that keeps rolling on his back may still be a bit too immature to train.)

D. Stop—Sit

To teach your dog to sit instantly on command during heelwork:

(*a*) step on to your left foot;
(*b*) place your left hand on the lead near your dog's neck;
(*c*) stop;
(*d*) draw him up, if necessary, and only as sharply as you feel he needs;
(*e*) say 'Jason, sit!';
(all simultaneously)
(*f*) reward him very warmly.

Once your dog is sitting promptly, there's no need to draw him up at all—just reward him warmly when he sits.

Don't do this more than about *once* per session—it tends to make a dog heel slowly in anticipation of a sit command.

1. *If he won't sit, or if he sits at his leisure*

Use the other end of the lead to sting him with at the *exact* instant you command him to sit, and reward him *instantly*. Repeat this as often as necessary (two or three times should do the trick). If he has a thick coat, instead of stinging him, give the check chain a sharp backward flick with your left hand. Only resort to this if you have to, though, as it's inclined to make a dog sit wide.

2. *If he sits just behind your legs*

If your dog always sits just behind you, he's probably anxious because you're tense. Crouch down, and he will come around. Stand up, and continue the lesson with warmer rewards, and keep relaxed. You can also try patting your leg just a little high—to encourage him to move around to reach your hand—and say 'Good dog!' lovingly, warmly and convincingly. You must, of course, pat his head when he comes all the way around to poke his nose under your hand—and praise him extravagantly for coming. If he's very anxious, touch him, withdraw your hand and repeat 'Good dog!' warmly.

Pat him only when he's in the correct position. Continue to work in a more relaxed manner, giving lighter corrections and warmer rewards.

3. *If he sits wide*

If your dog turns and sits at an angle (i.e. wide), shove him in with a slap on his buttocks, and say 'Good dog!' for sitting close. (Which, of course, he did nothing to merit.) You may have to do this repeatedly before he learns to sit close to you of his own accord.

4. *If he sits in front of your feet*

This is usually because:

(1) you're too slow to reward your dog for coming to the left side or for sitting. Your dog then noses around in front for his praise; or
(2) you're being too soft and not showing enough authority; or
(3) he's needing reassurance;
(4) or all three.

Praise and pat your dog the *very instant* he sits or comes into position at your left side—and if necessary smack his nose with your right hand to correct him if he still pushes around in front. Then continue, handling your dog with more authority.

E. Stop and Down

Dropping your dog alongside you as you walk is difficult and most dogs hate it. If you wish to do it, however, first refer to the chapter on teaching your dog to go down on command. When he's thoroughly familiar with this exercise, continue thus:

(1) walk your dog to heel;
(2) stop and say 'Jason, down!'; and
(3) let the lead go suddenly slack in front of him, bending slightly over him (when he's familiar with the exercise, you must remain upright);
(4) if he obliges, give him a loving reward;
(5) if he doesn't, either step on the lead sharply with your left foot beside his neck or push him down sharply at the back of his neck with your left hand holding his neck down until the rest of him goes down—and reward him.

Repeat this until he's learnt the exercise.

Do *not* do this exercise frequently. If your dog doesn't like it, and you can't teach him, don't persist with it. For some reason, although a dog knows he's in for a nasty correction, he'll still refuse to go down during the heel exercise, even though he knows perfectly well what's expected of him.

F. Walking to Heel off the Lead or Heeling Free

When you start walking with your dog off the lead, he may stay at your side very willingly—or he may take this opportunity to vanish.

If he won't stay with you, follow this procedure: Undo the catch, and immediately do it up again, throw your arms around your dog's neck and praise him as if he'd been extremely clever not to run away (although he hasn't had a chance). Walk him on the lead a while and repeat. Praise him profusely each time you reclasp the catch, acting as if he's achieved some brilliant feat. Increase the time you leave the lead undone *very* gradually. The idea is that he remains with you, eagerly anticipating the praise and hug he'll get when you redo the catch.

If he escapes, because he is taking a chance, and not because he is confused, either handle him with a rope, as described in the sit and stay exercise, or handle him thus: Be ready to step towards him and hit his disappearing buttocks hard with the metal end of the lead. Although it's unlikely that you'll get him back at this point by restoring trust—because he's probably hell-bent on getting to his kennel—crouch down to his level *instantly* you've hit him, keeping the lead behind your back out of sight, and try, he *may* come.

I wouldn't normally recommend using training equipment to correct a dog with—but we are dealing with a very spirited dog here. And if you're skilful, he won't see what hit him. If your dog is too quick for you, have an earth clod handy and throw that!

When you restore trust, crouch down immediately and drop the lead out of sight behind you. Your dog has the advantage of speed over you—you counter-attack with cunning—make him *want* to come!

If he doesn't come back *do not chase him*. Seek him out quietly, and when you find him—more than likely looking at you, remorseful and shamefaced, from his kennel, and tentatively wagging his tail—don't at this stage, punish him. Put the lead on him with a positive, authoritative attitude, and silently return to the lesson as if nothing had happened (resisting the urge to give the check chain a sharp jerk of revenge). Now make your rewards very warm, and don't unclasp the lead for some while. Make your lessons more fun—so that he has more incentive to stay, and don't make your lessons too long or too often—5 or 10 minutes daily at the most.

If it becomes a habit, however (not because your dog is confused but because he's a chancer) instead of leading him back meekly to his lesson, shake him till his teeth rattle. He has a high threshold, and it's not easy to reach. Try to get it through to him that it's fun and easy to work with you; it's no joke if he doesn't.

Don't lose your temper. Don't be tense. Handle him with warmth and intimacy on the one hand (although you could cheerfully throttle him) and authority on the other. Keep your lessons short and fun.

If your dog won't work without a lead, accept it—you're licked!

CHAPTER 13

COMING TO YOUR LEFT SIDE (THE FINISH)

To teach your dog to come around your back and position himself at your left side, do the following:

1. Place him on his lead, and hold the loop in your right hand. (Pass the lead from one hand to the other, as your dog goes around you.)
2. Stand with your dog across the back of your legs, as shown in Figure 1.
3. Keeping your feet in position, turn your body and look at your dog over your left shoulder.
4. Pat your side just high enough to be out of reach so that he has to come right around to get a pat on his head.
5. At the same time say 'Heel, boy!' in a bright, inviting tone of voice.
6. Before he moves, say 'Good dog!' warmly, *as if* he had actually come, even though he hasn't budged yet. This is to tempt him to come around for a pat.
7. Don't pet your dog until he has actually come *right* to your left side.
8. As he noses his way around, say '*That's* a good dog!' with the first movement he makes and encourage him verbally all the way around. (If he won't come, crouch down—that will bring him!)
9. When he's *at* your left side, give him a huge welcome, patting and hugging him and showing much delight. If, however, he wants to rush right across in front

of you, draw him up on the lead when he reaches the correct position—and reward him.

10. Do a half-turn, leaving him across the back of your legs again and repeat points 2–10 several times.

11. Then, position yourself as before, but let your left side be a little further out of reach from your dog, and repeat as before. (See Figures 2, 3 and 4.)

12. Repeat this a few times, each time letting your left side get a little further away from him, so that he has to come around a little further.

13. Turn slowly in a clockwise direction for a couple of seconds *as* your dog comes to your left side. Then stop and give him a big reward. This is to help him grasp the idea that he must come *around* your back to your left side.

While doing the above, adhere to these rules

(*a*) Keep your right hand out of reach or your dog may go to it and become confused.

(b) Let your voice carry over your left shoulder across your back to him.

(c) Reward him immediately after your command, before he even takes his first step to you.

(d) Don't touch him (unless he needs reassurance, then you withdraw your hand again), until he's in position. Only pet him when he has come all the way into position.

(e) Each time, while you're teaching your dog, reward him so that he thinks that to come around to your left side is a perfectly marvellous experience!

If you delay your reward when he comes to the left, he'll probably move around in front of you instead of taking up a *square* position at your left side.

When you've reached the stage where your dog moves around willingly from the position shown in Figure 5, tell him to sit and stay. Move two or three paces from him and, as you release him, pat your left side and say 'Heel, boy!' lightly. If he comes in front of you, push him gently over to the right and step forward, then restore trust across your back over your left shoulder, patting your side. If necessary, turn your left side a little towards him to guide him. Swivel your feet back to regain your former position as he comes around; and reward him.

Don't touch your dog until he's *at* your left side, or he won't see any reason why he should come all the way around. Practise this a few times.

If, after you release your dog from the stay position, he still refuses to come around on his own accord, and has to be pushed across every time, tap his nose when he comes in front of you, turn your body right around, speaking to him over your left shoulder, so that he can follow the direction of your voice, and quickly say 'Good boy!' warmly. Relieved to hear he's no longer in your bad books, he should dart around your back to your left side for his reward. If necessary, step forward after you've punished him, and if he won't come, crouch down.

If he comes and sits in front of you instead of coming around to your left side, don't just pat your side and say 'Heel!'—he won't come. *Step back*, pat your side and say 'Heel!' around your back. He's far more likely to come over the increased distance.

He may learn this in a few lessons or it may take much longer. If he doesn't come to the heel position at the end of one of his lessons, he may do so at the start of the next.

You'll be surprised how readily your dog adjusts to this position at your left side once he's learnt it, and automatically places himself there at any time of the day. If he finds a hand there and a quick pat, he'll be less likely to jump up against you.

Watch yourself for cheating! When your dog is not quite in position and you shuffle your feet around to make him square—you're only bluffing yourself!

1   2

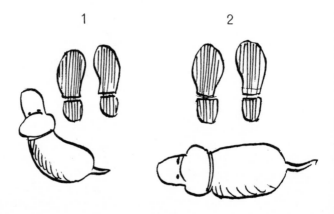

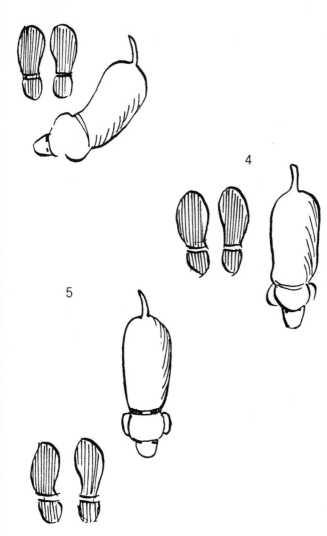

3

4

5

CHAPTER 14

THE DOWN COMMAND

Before you teach your dog the 'down' command, he should be completely familiar with the sit and stay exercise.

1. Place your dog on his lead.
2. Stand next to him.
3. Say 'Down!' in a firm voice.
4. Depending on his strength, either step on his check chain near his neck and press your foot decisively to the ground or put your hand on the back of his neck and push him down. Reward him and then let him get up again. If he places his 'elbows' on the ground, and arches his back, repeat 'Down!' and hold him there until he relaxes and goes down properly. Reward him.

   If you have a very powerful dog, and you're not strong enough, don't try, or you may injure your back. Either get someone stronger to help you or abandon the exercise.
5. Repeat this four or five times. When you push him down, always pat the side of his shoulder and reward him as warmly as if he'd gone down voluntarily.
6. Give your dog a break of a few minutes, going back to something he knows and enjoys, or give him a romp.
7. Repeat the down exercise a further four or five times, and give him another break.

8. If your dog is not going down of his own accord after this, either use the downward thrust of your foot as a correction, if you're using that method, or, if you're employing the other, smack him on his shoulders if he doesn't go down when you command him to. However, it's far easier to teach a dog to go down while he's running *to* you than it is to teach him from the sitting position, when he usually arches his back and resists.

You may achieve this in one lesson—or it may take you a few. Don't be in a hurry—go at your dog's pace.

To teach your dog to go down while he's moving towards you:
1. Put him on the lead.
2. Tell him to sit and stay.

3. Walk back three or four paces and face him.
4. Hold the loop of the lead in your outstretched left hand to prevent him from pulling back when you tell him to go down.
5. Release him.
6. Step forward on to your right foot.
7. Raise your right hand.
8. Command him sharply: 'Jason, down!'

Points 6, 7 and 8 must all be done simultaneously, and executed only when your dog's head is in the position illustrated in Figure 1 on page 256.

This is so that, should he ignore your command, you can push his head down sharply with your right hand (or, at a later stage, punish him with it). If his hind end won't go down, hold his head down until it does. Your left hand has the lead, so that, should he try to escape, you have him under control.

9. Let him run around after each 'down' command.

You can, instead of pushing his head down, put a foot forward on to a taut lead, pushing your foot down sharply between his forelegs—but this takes a little practice. Bend over and pat him on his shoulder each time you force him down.

When you feel he knows that he should go down when you give him the 'down' command, but still refuses, don't push him down; adjusting your punishment for him use your hand to smack the top of his head. You won't injure his tough skull with your hand, so don't worry! Rare is the dog that doesn't need this correction, they all take a chance, even when they know perfectly well what's expected of them.

Now that you've combined the 'Sit!' and 'Stay!' exercise with 'Down!', don't drop your dog on each occasion that you release him. In fact, don't drop him more than once in every five times you release him. In other words, tell him to sit and stay, and release him joyfully to you four times; then, on the fifth occasion, drop him before he reaches you. Otherwise, if you drop your dog too often, he'll start creeping forward, anticipating a drop command, instead of running joyfully to you when he's released.

DO NOT

(a) Command your dog before he's within reach (at this stage).

(b) Command him too late, when he's tangled up with your legs, and all that is left to punish is a backside. He'll probably leap up behind you, ready for more fun!

(c) Hesitate to punish him in the hope that he'll change his mind and oblige you. He won't.

(d) Ask him nicely to go down.

So far we've always had a hand above his head to punish him with if he doesn't go down instantly on command. Now, still holding the lead to control him with, drop him half a metre before he reaches his accustomed dropping position, as shown in Figure 2. But instead of keeping your hand suspended above his head when you command him, bring it down sharply and point to the ground. If he disobeys you, step forward and correct him. If he obeys you, step forward, pat him and praise him. He will, of course, pop right up when you do this, but that doesn't matter for the moment.

As you increase the distance at which you drop him, remove his lead.

Also, as the distance increases, say 'Down, stay!' Let him stay in the down position for a second, then praise him to release him and make a big fuss of him when he comes to you. Gradually increase the length of time he stays down, and the distance at which you drop him.

If he does not drop, walk up to him and correct him.

Over-correcting is very likely to make a dog run away

1

2

from the lesson. If he does this, give him lighter corrections. If, however, he's doing a bunk on you because he's a chancer, place him on a long lead as described for sit and stay. When he runs to the end of the lead and finds he can go no farther, point to the ground and say 'Down!' Realizing he has no option, he will (or he gets a bonk on the nut), whereupon you walk up to him, pat him warmly and say 'Good boy!' lovingly, to show him that it's not so bad after all.

Never lose your temper. Keep a balance between reward and reassurance; and authority and firmness. You must be firm enough to make him obey you, but loving enough to keep him from running from you. If you cannot achieve this balance, don't upset yoursel. and your dog by persisting with the exercise.

This exercise usually takes some weeks to teach, because dogs don't like it.

Keep the sessions very short, and your praise profuse, always praising your dog each time he goes (or is pushed) down.

If your dog really hates it, it would be better not to force him to do it. He may begin to hate his training altogether, which would be a pity.

Remember

1. When you're teaching your dog to go down, step and raise your hand simultaneously with your command. This step is very important. If necessary you can scrape your foot, making a noise, thus making the command still more forceful. (If training on sand or gravel.)
2. Have a firm and decisive attitude when you command.
3. Make your rewards cancel all the displeasure your dog derives from the command.
4. Don't hesitate when you need to correct your dog.
5. Don't drop him too often.
6. Keep your lessons short.

CHAPTER 15

TRAINING CLUBS, AND ADVANCED OBEDIENCE

Training Clubs

All training clubs are different. Some are too hard on their dogs, most are too soft and many not adaptable enough, saying that the dogs that can't be trained by their methods can't be trained at all. Some are friendly and others set in their ways, regarding newcomers with suspicion. Some regard their dog-training as lots of fun, others as the be-all and end-all of their existence. You can apply to the Kennel Club for a list of training clubs in your area.

It is a good idea not to teach your dog new exercises *at* your club, but at home where there are not so many distractions and criticisms.

When you join a club, don't try to mould your dog to their ways—and never let them tell you not to praise your dog! If you find a club that likes to look like a lot of two-legged zombies with four-legged zombies, walking around with long faces and never a word of thanks to their dogs (without whom they wouldn't be there anyway), 'enjoying' themselves, let them. Find a club with members that are more light-hearted, more ready to learn, and who really enjoy their dogs. If your dog doesn't enjoy being trained, what's the point?

Competitive Obedience

Any dog, any breed, any age and any shape, fully sexed or neutered, is allowed to enter the obedience ring.

Before entering your dog in an obedience show, he must be registered with the Kennel Club. If he's a mongrel, he can still be registered and compete against his blue-blooded cousins on the Obedience Register.

It is pleasing that mongrels are accepted to compete in the obedience ring. Dogs are, after all, bred for people— not people for dogs.

If you are wanting to teach your dog sendaway, scent discrimination, tracking, jumping and so on, I recommend Mollie Mulvany's book, *All about Obedience Training for Dogs*, published by Pelham Books. She has had vast experience and enormous success in competitive obedience and can take you further in advanced training. But should you become involved in advanced obedience work, build up your advanced training *slowly* and do it for pleasure—*not* to achieve perfection. You (and especially your dog) will get far more satisfaction out of it. Mollie has achieved top honours over and over again, and this is the approach that got her there.

Retrieving

I have been involved mainly in the training of problem dogs, and not dogs for obedience trials or sport. Mollie's book, and others, have dealt with this subject more comprehensively.

However, I do know that a lot of people have very little success when they try to teach their dogs to retrieve, either for fun at home or in obedience clubs.

From what I've seen, I'd say that, just as some people have a gift for playing the piano or painting pictures, some dogs have a 'gift' for guarding, retrieving, hunting and so on. A father who'd like his son to write a symphony can do his nut trying to force him, but if the boy is bent on being a mechanic he won't write a symphony—and it's the same with dogs. I've seen owners of dogs struggling endlessly to make their dog retrieve a dumb-bell. Sometimes they show infinite patience, sometimes red-hot fury—but their dog just doesn't understand.

While the owner shows his dog what to do—running with him on a lead to where he's thrown the ball or dumb-bell, and places it in his mouth (the dog's)—the dog looks vaguely around in puzzlement at what's going on!

If, after consulting another source on how to teach your dog to retrieve, your dog still doesn't grasp it, don't set your heart on achieving results, he may not be capable of learning it.

Retrieving slowly

However, if your dog retrieves, but comes in too slowly, correct this by allowing him to chase the dumb-bell while it's still moving. Don't make him wait at all after you've thrown it, but put him into playful spirits by allowing him to chase a moving object. In fact, *never* make him wait to retrieve—unless your judges are watching you!

It is unfortunate that obedience rules have thwarted a dog's natural instincts in retrieving—he should be allowed to *enjoy* his retrieving to the full! Only when you've made your dog retrieve quicker by letting him chase the dumb-bell, and praising him in by clapping your thighs, stimulating him, and so on, can you let him wait for his retrieve again. (Then he'll probably bring it in slowly all over again!)

Surrendering the dumb-bell

If your dog retrieves, but won't surrender the object, get it back from him thus: Go right down to his level and say 'Good dog!' very lovingly with infinite warmth and promise in your voice. But *don't* grab him as he draws close to you, or next time he'll skirt you with the dumb-bell in his mouth and a twinkle in his eye—and you're helpless! Simply praise him when he comes.

Do one thing at a time, concentrate first on getting him to *come* to you and praise him for it. Then pet him a while, tickle his chest and so on. Then, when he comes readily to you, concentrate on teaching him to *surrender* his dumb-bell. If, while he was a pup, you used to grab him when he came close to you, you're now reaping the troubles you sowed for yourself!

Never chase your dog, and never get cross with him—you'll just increase his fun—but if you go down to his level and talk nicely to him, keeping *completely* relaxed, he'll oon realize that you're not playing *his* game. Before you remove the dumb-bell, pet him, tickle his chest and so on, and then take it gently—and praise him.

When he finds out that prancing around with the dumb-bell *you're* after fails to produce the sport he so enjoyed, he'll come quicker on each occasion—especially if there's nice praise waiting for him! You have no other weapon—he has *four* legs, you have only *two*!

Always make it worth his while to give it up. When he comes—don't get tense or impatient. When he starts bringing it more readily, command him 'Leave!' or 'Drop it!', showing authority, *not* anger—if necessary, with a crisp verbal correction. When he finally lets go, show pleasure.

If, while you're playing at home with him, you're unable to recover your ball, stick, or dumb-bell, go indoors and leave him standing outside. With a little luck, if you do this often enough, he'll understand that the wisest course is to hand over, if he doesn't want his game to terminate! Otherwise get two or three balls—he can't hold them all!

Stand

To teach your dog to stand on command, place him in front of you. Say 'Stand!' as demonstrated, and lift him into a standing position, holding him under his tummy. To keep him there, gently tickle his tummy (he'll like it, so he'll stay) and praise him as if the effort were all his own!

Do this a few times, giving the check chain a slight jerk of encouragement, and praise him when he stands.

Then, tell your dog to sit. Stand in front of him and step back, telling him to stand—not sharply, but firmly as demonstrated. If he starts to take a step toward you, give him a light but crisp verbal correction with a forward step and a pointed finger.

Praise him for standing. Punishment in this exercise

is more likely to make a dog uncooperative, but by the time you've reached this exercise you should have developed a good relationship with your dog, and he shouldn't be needing much correction.

If your dog won't stand up from the sitting position, be patient. It's not an easy exercise to teach, because punishment will make him lie down, or step away from you—and you want to 'draw' him up. In order to make him stand on command, he *must* have confidence in you.

If your dog is being stubborn, say 'Jason, stand!' firmly, give the check chain a light jerk, pat your side and say 'Good boy!', *as if* he were standing, and continue as above. Do this two or three times per session until he has mastered the exercise. Any heavier correction than this will confuse him.

Show him often, be persuasive rather than authoritative, keep relaxed, and give your dog ample reward. Try to master a balance of authority—that keeps your dog from stepping toward you; and trust—that makes him want to obey you.

Distant Control

This is such a difficult exercise that even after I have taught a dog distant control and he's doing it from 10 metres, and his owner has *watched* me teach him, and received instructions from me personally over and over again, he simply can't get his dog (that knows the exercise off pat) to do it!

If you haven't the knack, you can't acquire it by learning—let alone by means of a book! If you can't master it, don't blame your dog—don't even blame yourself. Just don't upset your dog by having your heart set on teaching him—it's a difficult exercise.

You have taught your dog to sit, go down and, perhaps, to stand. Now you must combine these, first from at his side, then from a pace in front of him and then a couple of metres away from him.

Start teaching your dog this when his training is well advanced, and *don't* upset him with it. It would be a pity to undo all your other work, and spoil his confidence at the same time, just because of this exercise.

To teach your dog distant control

(1) Stand next to him and tell him to go down, pointing to the ground.
(2) Bend down and pat him, saying 'Good dog!'
(3) Pat your side and tell him to sit up, as described in the sit and stay exercise. (When you give this command from in front of him, hold your hand out slightly lowered, palm turned up, and as you give your command, flick your fingers up and raise your hand in a manner that suggests to him he must sit up. Do this with firmness, patience, and kind authority.)
(4) Praise him.
(5) Take a small step forward and tell him to stand.
(6) Praise him.

... an article of clothing ...

Now try from the front, standing upright, with one foot forward. Here you require that subtle control that keeps your dog's confidence, and yet keeps him from coming to you—or running away.

Each time he changes position, step forward and pat him (unless he's highly excitable) and tell him to stay. As he masters it, instead of praising each change in position, he can see your approval on your face, and he gets extravagant praise when the whole business of getting up and down is over!

Keep quite a space of time between each change in position—because so often the dog, once he's learnt, he stands, sits, lies down, and so on without being given any command! But he's trying to please, and that's *all* that matters—he's not a computer, he's an animal!

Your training club will show you what hand signals they use.

Sendaway

I can particularly recommend Mollie Mulvany's method for the sendaway. It is an exercise dogs hate. And we don't like making our dogs do what they so dislike. But she has developed an approach that the dogs actually *enjoy*.

This is what she suggests: Put down an article of your clothing. Stand a pace away from it. Your dog knows to go into his basket to lie down, so point to it and tell him, first, the command your club uses for sendaway ('Away', for instance) and then 'Basket' or 'Lie down'. But say it nicely, lightly and pleasantly. When he does, bend over, pat him, praise him warmly, step back and release him.

Slowly increase the distance, always letting your dog think he's very clever to go and lie on your clothing! Always *go* to him to praise him, so that he doesn't develop the habit of coming to you for his praise as soon as he's been dropped in the advanced stages of the exercise.

When he associates 'Away' with 'Basket' or 'Lie down'—you need only say 'Away' to command him. Remember—command kindly, but firmly. When he reaches the article, say 'Down' nicely to him—he's going to lie down anyway, so you don't have to command him sharply.

When your dog goes readily to his target from about 10 metres (this may take weeks to achieve—the slower you go, the more fun you make it for him, and the less you upset him, the sooner he'll learn it), start gradually diminishing the size of the article until you've removed it altogether—and, when he reaches the exact spot where it was, drop him, with, if necessary, a little more authority. He'll probably be a little perplexed, so tell him to stay, go to him and let him think he has just done the most wonderful thing a dog ever did! He'll be very ready to repeat the praise, again, so take him back lightheartedly, and send him to the same spot again—from the same position—repeating as before. Now leave it until the next lesson.

Let all your lessons be short, and at the *most* once a day.

Now find a new site—*with* your clothing, and start *all over again*, right from telling him to go and lie down, a few paces from the article.

Never let your dog be confused—let him have a *purpose* and *reason* to go away from you, and a target to *go to*. It is without these that dogs dread the send-away.

When you're not in the ring, skip and bound up to him after he's been dropped to praise and hug him. *That*, in his mind, is what it's all about! When you're in the ring hold him with your eyes, and do the praising etc. when you're in private!

If you have to redirect him, do this gently and care-fully—it is *far* more important that he *tries* than that he is right.

Let your club guide you further, but *don't* let them make you upset your dog. He's *your* dog, and he's an individual, and you know which training methods he responds to best.

Manwork

This, of course, you can't do without the correct equipment which a club that undertakes manwork will have.

No dog should attempt manwork unless he has reached a very high standard of obedience.

Some dogs are completely uninterested and others take to it like a duck to water.

Some are uninterested because they are still a bit young, and the potential must yet develop. Others need to watch other dogs working for a while before they click what it's all about—and others have not the potential, and never will.

Some dogs are intelligent enough to distinguish the real thing from an artificial situation, and even if the dog doesn't take the arm he will still defend his master in real danger. The fact that he won't attack in sport may be a disappointment, however, but the dog is really worth owning. His mature disposition will reveal his potential to a discerning owner.

Too much manwork, however, can become boring to even an enthusiastic dog who is constantly being told to leave, just when he's really beginning to enjoy the attack!

CHAPTER 16

TRAINING A DOG
FOR THE SHOW RING

When a dog enters the show ring, he must walk nicely on his lead, allow strangers to approach and handle him, not try to fight and play with every dog he sees, and, if possible, stand on command.

While your pup is tiny, place him on a table once a day, and handle him gently. This is what he will experience when he's big enough to compete for show honours. If you speak nicely to him while you handle him, never *force* him to do anything, and let him enjoy the experience, he'll be much more likely to co-operate when the judges handle him. Ask your friends to do this for you as well (provided they're never rough) to help him get used to being handled by people he doesn't know.

It is also important that a dog doesn't come straight out of a kennel or a sheltered environment for the first time slap into the middle of a show ring, when he's never even seen other dogs before, let alone the bustle, noise and crowds of a dog show. Next thing, the judges want to see his teeth and walk around him in circles. In his bewilderment, he'll probably come bottom of the class, whereas, had he been introduced gradually to crowds, he may have walked off with first prize.

1. *If your dog withdraws* when a judge approaches him, help him to overcome it in the following way.

Teach him to stay on command in the stand position. Be calm and firm—showing neither anger nor sympathy. Don't let your dog stand right next to you while he's being handled, but a couple of paces away, so that he hasn't got a convenient pair of legs right next to him to hide behind. When he looks at you while he's being handled, stand upright and keep a firm expression on your face—eyes that say 'stay' will hold him. Immediately afterwards, let him come for reassurance. The knowledge that there's a kind pat after his ordeal will help him through it. Practise this with friends before he goes into the ring again.

2. *If your dog tries to go after other dogs* in the ring, be sharp with him, but remember that you are going against nature—it's hard for him. Reward him warmly every time he resists chasing other dogs and let him always find a hand to pat him, and make it worth his while, and you'll have a much better chance of controlling him.

3. *If, every time a judge handles your dog, he just folds up*, don't get cross with him, he'll only crumple up twice as fast next time.

Practise at home with him, and when he collapses just

pretend nothing has happened, put your hand under his tum, lift him gently into the position you want him in, and praise him lightly and warmly. The idea is to make him think that he's very clever to stand properly, and you *must* let him think that! If patience, gentleness, firmness and warm praise don't get him right—nothing will, and you'll just have to accept it, he's not cut out for fame and fortune!

4. *If your dog won't let you look at his teeth*, handle him thus: touch his mouth with all the seriousness of a judge inspecting his teeth, hesitate, then throw your arms around his neck and tell him he's marvellous!

He'll love this. The idea is to make him anticipate this praise. Lift his lip just slightly—and repeat. Hold his bottom jaw gently, and touch his upper lip—and reward him! If you do this for about a minute a day, over the weeks, he'll soon be letting you look in his mouth. Because he will become so eager for his hug, he won't struggle. But if he *does* struggle—clobber him! (But not too hard!) Say 'No!' and smack his nose, then firmly and gently repeat, hesitate a shorter time, even if it's only for one second—and reward him. Keep your sessions very short, and have a game after each one. Don't do it too often.

I don't think you've much chance of getting the judge to reward him as *you* do, so gradually get him used to having his teeth inspected without his bonus before he next goes into the ring.

5. *If your dog rolls over on to his back* when you want to show him, he is probably a little too young for such a serious business. If you don't wait until he's mature before showing him again, you may become so impatient with his nonsense that you'll never be able to show him.

If he is a mature dog and rolls over on to his back, refer to the section on heelwork for handling a dog that adopts this vice. But instead of walking with him when he gets up, tell him to 'Stay!' (not too sharply or he'll crumple again). Inspect him for a second and praise him. Then continue as described above for a dog that won't allow his teeth to be inspected.

Don't give your dog chocolates and biscuits and what-not in the show ring. Treat him as if he's a personality, and not a machine that needs oiling. Develop a relationship with him; teach him to be obedient, and enjoy pleasing you, so that you can enjoy the show ring together.

On show days, find shade for your dog, and give him as much water as he needs—he'll get very thirsty. Give him exercise from time to time, while he's waiting for his turn in the ring, and before home time.

Let your dog be first and foremost a pet, regardless of his merit or otherwise in the ring—he honestly can't help what he looks like any more than *you* can! If they were judging on which was the most loving, loyal dog with the finest personality—he'd certainly win!

CHAPTER 17

DELINQUENT DOGS

1. Not coming when called

Dogs that don't come when they're called are sorted out in chapter 10.

2. Over-exuberance

Page 46 will help you decide whether or not your dog is suitable for you. Consider now whether or not you have enough space for him.

If you feel either that you'll never be able to handle him or that he's too confined, see chapter 18 on how to set about finding a more suitable home for your dog. Unfortunately, people rarely follow this advice because, even though their dogs are quite out of hand, they love them too much to part with them. Then, not only are their dogs insecure without proper handling, and frustrated without adequate space, but their owners' lives are made intolerable by their excessive high spirits.

However, you may decide that you and your dog *are* compatible and that you have the space to keep him, in which case the problem is actually quite easily dealt with.

Handle your dog with authority and decisiveness, as described in the section on correction and reward. Never shout at him, threaten him, despair, get frustrated or angry. Simply command him, punish him, reward him, and assert your authority over him.

And—*most* important—give your dog a proper outlet for his energy by exercising him daily off the lead.

A well-conducted training programme will also give

your dog a sense of right and wrong. It will make him
get into the habit of restraining himself; and it will teach
him to enjoy pleasing you. He probably has quite a high
threshold of correction.

3. Jumping up

When your dog jumps up against you, be very firm
with him. As he jumps up, say 'Don't jump!' sharply
(don't say 'Down!' if you're training him, or he'll confuse his commands) and correct him. The best way to
correct him is to thrust your knee up sharply into his
chest to wind him slightly. If this is too difficult, smack
his face. If he's large and persistent and you're not much
of a match for him, take off your shoe and let him feel
the heel of that.

If your punishment is effective he'll be upset. It is
therefore imperative that you put your hands down
immediately for him to come to them. Pet him when he

comes—while he' has all four feet on the ground. When you take your hands away, command: 'That's enough!', and punish any further attempt he makes to jump up again. Now (1) step away from your dog; (2) keep your hands down so that he can come to them; (3) call him quietly to you, and (4) repeat the procedure if he jumps up again. *But* reward him very warmly when he starts heeding you (be careful not to stimulate him).

If your dog is trained to come to the left side, tell him 'Don't jump!', call him to the heel position, and give him his greeting when he is sitting in that position. If he's small, pick him up. When you put him down again after his greeting, repeat the command 'Don't jump!'

Next time he comes running to you to jump up against you, step towards him, point a threatening finger at him, and say 'Don't jump!' He probably will, so repeat the procedure of punishing him and putting your hands down for him to come to them. Sooner or later, he'll hesitate, anticipating his correction; when he does, *put your hands down instantly* because, if you don't, he'll jump up to seek them. This is vital if you're hoping to teach your dog not to jump up—let him have a hand to come to.

You won't always have to give your dog the command: 'Don't jump!'—but you'll always have to put a hand down to pat him with when he comes to greet you. If he doesn't find a hand, up he'll jump. That's one of the inconveniences of owning a lively dog—dog comes, hand down.

Some dogs, when they discover what happens to them when they jump up and lick their owners' faces, decide it's safer to do it from behind. An extrovert dog like this takes a heavy punishment and this habit can only be broken by catching him a backward kick—crude as it sounds, and following the same procedure of 'Don't jump!' and restoring trust.

4. Nervousness

A dog may be nervous because he has inherited his nervousness from one or both of his parents; because he is too inbred; because of some frightening experience he may have had; because he has a highly strung owner; or because he's led an over-sheltered life.

If his nervousness is extreme, his life is one living hell and he should be put to sleep, where he has no more terrors to torment him every day. The noise and bustle of modern life—phones ringing, radios, traffic, raised voices and clanging of household activities—are all too much for him. Allowing him to live is as cruel as any deliberate act of cruelty.

A dog that's not very nervous, however, may benefit from a carefully planned training programme. He should be handled patiently and lovingly, firmly and decisively, with barely any punishment, other than verbal correction. If he's amply rewarded, the pride he develops through his achievement should boost his confidence. Decisiveness is important—sympathy creates self-pity, and kind decisiveness gives confidence.

Should your dog be so nervous that he draws away from you, and won't let you touch him, to get him to come to you, crouch down and speak to him in low tones. (Low tones give a nervous dog confidence; raised tones increase his nervousness.) Once you've fixed his attention, reach out your hand lovingly, and continue speaking to him. As he draws near (or, as you reach out and touch him), tickle his tummy or scratch behind his ears before you lift him, put his lead on him or whatever you're wanting to do with him. *Never* chase, grab or corner a nervous dog. With patience, as described, it's easier than you would think, to get him to come to you. Handle him firmly and positively. Be in no hurry, and remain completely relaxed.

If you have a dog that is afraid of a raised hand, and constantly expects to be hit, put him on a lead. (If he plays up, see later in the chapter, on how to handle a dog that resists a lead.)

Hold the lead short and firmly in your left hand, and handle your dog positively, firmly and lovingly. Do not allow him to back away further than the end of the lead, or his fear will increase. Raise your right hand in a slightly threatening gesture, then bring it down, neither slowly nor quickly, but in a natural manner, to both caress *and* reward him. If your dog flinches, the caress and reward will come as a pleasant surprise. Speak lovingly to him while you do this. Do it once a day, and after several days or weeks the fear of being struck should, to a certain extent, be removed. But these experiences, unfortunately, implant themselves indelibly in a dog's mind, and can seldom be completely eradicated.

Some otherwise confident dogs become nervous through leading an over-protected and sheltered life. If, for instance, your dog is having a walk in the park and

another dog approaches him, or something startles him, causing him to shoot his tail under and run for cover, even mentioning his name will reinforce his fear. But if he's left *entirely alone*, without any sympathy, to creep back and investigate on his own, his courage will develop as he finds out for *himself* that things are, after all, not so terrifying.

Nervousness is often hereditary and for this reason it's not a good idea to breed from a nervous dog, as it only produces more nervous dogs. More often than not, these dogs are too inbred. Intensive inbreeding lowers a dog's stamina—both mentally and physically—until the dogs become unfit to cope with the demands of living, and do not make very suitable pets.

5. Fear of noises and encouraging a dog not to be gun-shy

It's very difficult, if at all possible, to cure a dog of a fear of noises. However, the following procedure may help a dog to overcome this fear.

Play your dog's favourite game, stimulating him to a high pitch of excitement while someone lets off a popgun, a toy gun or an air gun, once or twice at some distance, so that he can only just hear it. Gradually increase the number of times it's let off, and bring it slowly nearer the dog each time you play so that after several weeks it's about 5 metres away from him. If you try to go any faster, you'll simply make him *more* afraid. Let the gun off about three or four times at each session.

Do this once a day, but never terrify your dog. Remember that it's perfectly natural for any dog to be afraid of a very loud noise.

On Guy Fawkes night, dogs should be shut indoors, whether or not they're afraid of noises. Any vet or animal clinic can tell you of the casualties they deal with at this time of the year. If your dog is afraid of the noise, the vet can give him a tranquillizer and you can also draw

the curtains, close the windows and turn up the radio to help drown the sound of the crackers.

If your dog is afraid of thunder I don't think there is anything you can do to help him overcome it, except perhaps, if he is over-sheltered, give him more outings, and help drown the sound, as described above.

6. Biting

Why do dogs bite? A dog may bite, for instance, if he is in pain; he may have been bred from parents that are vicious; if your dog is a bitch, she may be guarding her young; the dog may be nervous; he may have been ill-treated or teased; he may be bored and releasing pent-up energy, or, as is most often the case, he is over-protective. (Puppies that bite are dealt with in chapter 2 in the section on play.) A dog that has hair growing over his eyes may also bite because he can't see properly.

(1) If your dog bites only when he's touched in a certain area, he may have earache, an abscess or some painful spot that needs attention. If he bites while he's being groomed, you may be hurting him and should therefore be more patient and gentle with him, and if necessary, more firm.

(2) However, if your dog bites only when you attempt to punish him, you're probably under-punishing him and he needs severe correction for this. If he's on a lead, hold it against the side of his face to prevent his biting you again, and then punish him with one or two sharp and effective corrections. If he's not on a lead, shake him until his teeth rattle—then restore trust.

(3) Some dogs have a rather endearing habit of either 'talking' in the back of their throat, or curling up their lips and showing their teeth—'smiling'. It may appear rather alarming to anyone who's not familiar with dogs, but the contented expression on the face of the first dog, and the wagging tail of the second, make it easy to distinguish between this display of pleasure and viciousness.

(4) When a dog attacks, it is either premeditated, and can be controlled, as in the case of a dog that's protecting his master or property, or it is a reflex action, and is very difficult to control, as in the case of a dog that's been teased or is attacking someone screaming, running or becoming hysterical.

I don't think a person who's afraid of a dog does, in fact, give off a smell. He either panics and precipitates this reflex, or has an unnatural, tense attitude which the dog may interpret as a threat—and therefore bites. Anyone afraid of being attacked should, in fact, relax, as this reflex will be much less likely to be triggered off.

I've seen the same dog viciously attack a screaming, hysterical person *and*, on another occasion, try desperately to get a grip on someone else who remained indifferent—either because he was drunk, or knew the ways of dogs! And haven't we all seen, at one time or another, a dog pounce on a cat and then become quite perplexed when she glances at him over her shoulder, puts her tail in the air and strolls away—nine times out of ten, unharmed! This is a natural behaviour pattern in a dog. In the wild state, when dogs fight for superiority, the one that surrenders ceases to fight or defend himself rolling on his back in an attitude of surrender. This triggers a reaction in the superior dog, which causes him to cease attacking.

We often see a pup, when he's apprehensive, roll on his back in an attitude of surrender. He is displaying the same behaviour pattern—but on the receiving end this time.

If a dog is vicious to the extent that he is attacking, either as a result of ill-treatment or teasing, or as a result of inherited viciousness, he should on no account be allowed to live. If he's kept out of harm's way, his life won't be worth living. You'll either have to close him away or chain him up, and his life will be deadly dull. Moreover, you'll be constantly worrying whether he's going to get free and attack someone.

Muzzles are uncomfortable for a dog, because he can't pant when he exerts himself—and not completely effective. Those jaws are really strong, and the leather muzzle does not contain them adequately when an attacking dog really means business. Castrating him isn't likely to remove such a deep-seated desire to attack, and training him is also futile. Even if he's trained to the point where he obeys like a computer, then overtrained, so that his spirit is broken, the last thing he'll surrender before his life will be his urge to attack.

However, if your dog's biting is not too severe, he should be sharply corrected for any attempt he makes to bite. Firstly, whenever possible, remove any source of irritation (if, for instance, children are teasing him, they, too, must be disciplined); then, each time he snarls or snaps, bring a hard object (the flat edge of a ruler or a coat-hanger, for instance) down sharply on to his nose (in the case of a noseless breed, the top of his head).

A dog's scent organs are so protected from damage by his bone structure that you can be sure his nose will come to less harm than anyone at the receiving end of his teeth would! Then step back and restore trust. Thereafter punish him severely for any further growl or attempt to bite. Repeat the situation he disliked, and then reward him *very warmly* for the restraint he will show — if the punishment was sufficient. Do not, however, expect your dog to continue to restrain himself if he is allowed to be teased or unreasonably annoyed.

If your dog is biting you because you're going too near his food, or trying to take a bone from him, he can, if he's young enough, be taught in the same way to be more tolerant.

(5) Nervous snapping can be handled as described above for nervous flinching. If, instead of flinching, your dog snaps at your hand, be decisive and ignore his nipping. Nervous nippers seldom hurt — he shouldn't hurt you if you don't try to pull away from him. A training programme, carefully carried out, should give him more confidence and teach him to restrain himself.

But if your dog is constantly afraid and nipping in terror, it would be kinder to put him to sleep.

(6) A dog may also nip if he's an intense dog. A very intense dog that nips when he gets over-excited doesn't even know he's doing it, so it's not easy to cure. He needs more attention and intense affection, but is seldom completely satisfied. More attention and firm handling may possibly cure him but, if it doesn't, have him put down. Such an intense dog is a very unhappy dog.

(7) Sometimes a dog may suddenly start biting

strangers for no apparent reason. He's probably an intelligent dog without enough to amuse and occupy him. If your dog starts biting out of boredom, you'll probably cure him if you allow him indoors, give him plenty of companionship, supervised exercise and a training programme. The latter will be an outlet for his intelligence and will also teach him to restrain himself.

(8) Most dogs, however, bite because they are protecting their owners. It is their very quality that is their downfall—*Alsatians* for example, are conscientious protectors, and therefore bite innocent passers-by who, they think, are a threat to their family. Visiting children may also get bitten when they play roughly—the dog thinks his own family are getting hurt and takes action to protect them.

Any breed of dog can take up this kind of biting, and the desire to protect should not be discouraged, but controlled. The dog should, of course, be trained. Because this type of biting is not a reflex, but a pre-meditated action, it *can* be brought under control, if handled correctly.

The dog must be handled with decisiveness, firmness and authority. When he has learnt to 'Leave!', on command, and resists the temptation to make a meal of someone coming near his beloved owner, a hand to pat his head in appreciation for this self-control will reinforce his obedience.

When he is properly trained, he shouldn't bite, unless his owner is actually under attack, or on the command of his owner. This self-control develops naturally during a well-conducted training course. The dog should not, of course, have access to the street, or be near children when they play roughly, and a notice should be put on the gate warning people of his presence.

Anyone with a dog like this and who has not the strength of character to match his dog's determined efforts to protect, should carefully find a more suitable owner for the dog (see next chapter).

(9) Lastly, there is a kind of 'biting' that seems to worry some people. The dog mouths his owner's hand gently, and his owner sometimes fears that this will turn into biting. But it is a totally different behaviour pattern which will never turn into vicious biting—the dog is just trying to express his love. If he does it too roughly, he should be corrected; if he does it too often, he's probably needing more attention—and perhaps, discipline.

7. Fighting

Small dogs often have spirit and guts to compensate for what they lack in stature and this often leads to a belligerent attitude towards all bigger dogs. The bigger dog usually looks embarrassed for a while, and then, when he can take no more, he puts the cocky little blighter in his place. And who comes off second best? To control this situation, firstly, teach you dog to come when he is called, secondly keep him in, and lastly, supervise his exercise.

You won't cure him, and I doubt if you'll cure the chronic bully of the neighbourhood. What was said above of dogs that attack people applies to fighting dogs as well. Removal of parts, back and fore, may help, but that fighting spirit nearly always remains after all mutilation and training.

For punishment to be effective, it must exceed the intensity of the excitement created by the situation. You'll find no punishment effective, because a dog is quite oblivious to pain in the excitement of a fight.

However, if his fighting habit has not established itself too deeply, a strict training programme may develop his self-control enough to cure him—especially if he's still young.

If you'd like to try to teach your dog to stop picking fights, you can try the following programme: Put him on a lead. Hold it short and keep your elbow in. (This gives you maximum control over your dog.) Hold a sturdy stick in your right hand and as he dives for another dog, say 'Leave!' and wallop him across the nose and draw him up instantly very sharply. Step back and restore trust.

You may need to do this a few times before your dog stops attacking other dogs, and the most you're ever likely to achieve is that he'll look at you when he feels the urge to attack. If you're quick on the uptake and reward him profusely (if you go down and step back to make *him* come to *you* for his reward, you'll have his full attention) he'll not attack—provided you're around. Count yourself lucky if you get that far!

If you have a dog that fights, he should never be allowed out without the supervision of an adult. Children may get bitten when trying to rescue their pet from a fight, or your dog may kill or injure a small dog—or take on one too big for him to handle! (See separating a dog fight on page 96.)

If you have two dogs in the home that fight, give a training programme to the one that starts the trouble. If this doesn't cure them, you shouldn't keep them both. Leaving them to fight it out will cause them too much injury and they'll always hate each other—to say nothing of the impossible situations created in the home by trying to keep them apart, and the resulting frayed nerves. I give this advice with my tongue in my cheek, because I know no one ever takes it! But it really is advice worth taking. Which dog do you give away? You love them both! But what a relief it will be when one has gone to a new home, and if the home is carefully chosen the dogs will be so much happier.

. . . a belligerent attitude

8. Chasing cars

A dog should not be allowed off the lead where there is traffic and so should never develop the habit of chasing cars. Some people believe in frightening a dog out of this kind of behaviour but that is really not satisfactory. Always keep your dog under control on or near roads.

A dog either starts chasing cars because he's bored, because he copies another dog, or, as in the case of *Corgis* or *Border Collies*, because of the urge to chase moving objects. His strong muscles and pent-up energy are seeking an outlet, and an alternative (games or walks) will have to be provided.

Once you deny your dog this excitement, you'll have to fill the vacuum left by giving him proper exercise, playing with him and giving him companionship. If possible, he should also have a well-conducted training programme to develop his sense of self-discipline and, because a dog is an intelligent animal that hates to be bored, it provides a challenge for his intelligence.

9. Digging gardens and chewing plants

A dog digs in the garden for the same reason that he chases cars. He's bored. Handle this problem from both angles as well. But you'll find this crime much easier to cure.

If the criminal is a pup, you can't punish him unless he's caught in the act otherwise he won't understand. Reprimand him and give him a shaking. After three or four such corrections, he should drop the habit. But the next time he's allowed to become bored, it may be the washing on the line, instead of the garden, that will suffer!

However, if the culprit is an adult dog, you won't have to catch him in the act. Even if it's a couple of hours after he's dug a hole, you can still take him to it, correct him and tell him you heartily disapprove of what he's done. He's not stupid—he'll know who dug that hole (or chewed that plant). Next time he does it (as he surely will), take him back, reprimand him and correct him more severely.

Hereafter, any further digging sessions can be punished with both sharp words, *and* earth rubbed in his mouth—until he stops. You can be sure that he will, because he'll come to hate the taste of soil.

What may happen after a while is that when he's done some gardening he'll hide from you. If he's a big dog, it'll be difficult to catch him and drag him to the scene of the crime. If he's too big to drag to his hole, rub soil into his mouth—wherever it is that you find him. He'll get the message.

However, don't chase him in temper—he can run faster than you. Be careful not to show you're angry *until* you've found and secured him. This way you'll avoid a chase and a hunt. (But don't *call* him to you for his punishment either, or he won't come to you next time you want him. Find him, walk up to him, rub soil in his mouth and drop the subject.)

10 Chewing household effects

This can be devastating to carpets, new shoes, favourite toys and antique furniture.

Should you find your dog has been exercising his teeth on your property, show him the ruined object, give him blazes and correct him with a shaking or smack his nose as severely as you feel his temperament and age will permit—and give him a marrow bone and toys to exercise his teeth on.

He may also be needing more exercise and attention. If he's old enough, a well-conducted training programme will also help.

11. Lying on furniture

Sit on a chair for a while, then sit on the floor for a while, and you'll know why you find your chair curiously warm when you come home. Your dog, lying on the floor, is the picture of innocence—having heard your car, or footstep, which always warns him in time to hop off quick.

If you're lucky enough to catch your dog stretched out in your favourite armchair, tell him what you think of him and correct him. If you're not—close the living-room door, or put a sheet on his favourite chair when you go out.

If your dog's basket or bedding is always accessible to him, you'll have a better chance of winning the battle.

12. Reverting to unclean puppy habits and soiling the lawn

Messing indoors is against a dog's instinctive behaviour, but a relapse may be precipitated by his being unable to get outside on one or two occasions; he may be incontinent; he may not have enough opportunity to relieve himself at night, he may have an emotional upset, or, if he doesn't come inside very often the excitement of being let indoors may precipitate a reflex—and he makes a puddle. When coming inside is no longer such a novelty, this will, of course, right itself.

If your dog is getting old (especially if she's a spayed bitch) and messes indoors, it may be that she is incontinent, and the action is therefore uncontrollable. The vet can give her hormone injections which will enable her to control her bowel and bladder action again.

(Although this is more common in bitches, it is also possible that a male dog could suffer the same lack of bowel and bladder control when he starts ageing.)

Should this not be the case, however, an adult dog, unlike a pup, can remember afterwards who's responsible for that puddle or otherwise on the carpet.

Take your dog to it, point to it and show him your disapproval; he'll probably feel terribly ashamed and will probably need no further correction. Although he's unlikely to repeat his misdemeanour, he may need to be reprimanded a few times if the habit has become firmly established. Physical correction is not usually necessary.

Carpet experts assure us that soda-water applied after the urine has been sponged completely neutralizes any harmful effects the dog's urine may have on your carpet. Put this on immediately, so that it leaves no mark. However, to remove the odour completely, put pepper on the spot after it's been cleaned up so that your dog doesn't go back to it.

If you feed your dog at midday or in the morning, he will also find it easier to be clean at night.

A dog that's simply put out at night, then let in again ten minutes later, has probably spent the whole time waiting at the door to be let in again—and then does what he was meant to on the kitchen floor during the night.

But if he's taken for a short walk, before being put to bed at night, he'll be prompted to relieve himself by all

. . . all that's required . . .

the scents he picks up on the outing. He may do all that's required within a few seconds, but some dogs don't empty their bladders completely until they've lifted their leg a dozen times! And you'll both enjoy the walk in the evening anyway.

Reverting to unclean puppy habits can also be a sign that a dog is unhappy about something. A change in domestic routine that affects him adversely, a family upset, not enough attention, too strict a training programme, and so on, can all cause a dog to start messing indoors again. This is not unlike bedwetting in a child, where punishment simply makes the problem worse. Removal of the upset wherever possible, together with the above instructions, should correct the problem.

If your dog soils the lawn, he's probably not getting his daily walk. A dog that's taken for a walk at reasonably regular hours usually saves his motions to relieve himself away from home. (Sometimes *he'll* go next door, and the next-door dog will come to *your* lawn!) If your dog still soils the lawn in spite of regular outings, regard keeping the lawn clean as one of the inconveniences of owning a dog.

There is also another aspect to this problem—the male dog that cocks his leg at every pillar and post, be it your best chesterfield suite or your front door. This is an instinctive behaviour pattern and not easy to eradicate. If you're hoping to cure your dog, you *must* catch him in the act, and the punishment must be severe.

Sometimes a dog wees when he's petted or corrected. This must never be punished—the dog doesn't even know he's doing it. If you do, he'll just do it more. If your dog puddles when he's being petted, handle him more gently, give him more attention, and, as he gets more confidence, it will right itself. If he does it when he's being punished, he's being overcorrected and perhaps not getting enough attention.

13. Eating stools (Excrement)

To break a dog of this habit, firstly see that he has a balanced diet. Then put pepper on all the stools you can get to before he does, until he begins to leave them alone. Some dogs start this habit because they are too confined, and should obviously be given more freedom.

14. Pulling on the lead

This is much easier to correct than you'd ever imagine!

Read the chapter on Come on Command and see to it that, firstly, it's *very exciting* for your dog to *stay* at your side and not to pull (getting rewarded, patted, chatted to, and so on), and secondly, that he finds it most unpleasant if he does pull. (Chapter 12 will guide you on punishing your dog when he pulls on the lead.) If your dog finds you 'nice to be near', you've won half the battle. Secondly, exert your authority over him, giving him sharp commands and either sharp jerks on the check chain or sharp verbal corrections when he wants to run ahead.

When your dog pulls, never let your arm become outstretched—this will give him maximum control over you. To have maximum control over *him*, keep your elbow in and keep the lead short, using your heels to resist him. From there, let the instructions in chapter 10 guide you on how to control him on a lead which you will keep hanging loose (while he's still on the end of it!).

However, no dog can be exercised adequately on a lead. The lead should only be used when he's being taken out on roads, but try to find a safe open space where he can run free. Even if you're an Olympic athlete, a large healthy dog on a lead will be bursting for a run after *you* have walked to the point of exhaustion!

... pulling on the lead ...

15. Refusing to go on a lead

(a) *If your dog refuses to budge*

If your dog digs in his heels as soon as he has a lead on him, don't hold the other end, but run ahead of him, play with him, sit and pat your thighs so that he drags the lead as he runs to you. Perhaps you can let him have a walk with his lead dragging on the ground. (If he's likely to get into any trouble, lengthen it so you can step on it.)

He may learn to accept a lead if he always has something to walk *to*—a morsel, or perhaps someone he loves—or perhaps he will run eagerly to an open car door.

Once he starts forgetting about the fact that someone's holding his lead—let him *enjoy* going for a walk. Pat your side, chat to him brightly, praise him, trot along with him, and always let him enjoy the scents he finds on his walk.

(b) *If he 'does his thing', bucking and rolling*

If your dog has had a bad experience on a lead, he may never adjust to one. If he's a small dog, he may accept a harness. But this he should wear only on outings.

If your dog screams and does contortions when he's put on a lead—*not* because he has been previously ill-treated, but because he just doesn't like it—handle him thus:

Hold your end of the lead very firmly, with confidence and authority. Keep relaxed—and don't show any despair at your dog's 'unreasonable' antics. Don't let the lead go, and don't let him pull you even one pace. If he's very strong, keep your elbow in and use your whole body-weight against him.

Crouch or sit on the ground (this is because it is an unthreatening position and will give him easy access to your face, which he'll like) while he gets on with his antics. *Give him no command whatsoever* and *do not* move towards him. Speak reassuringly to him and say 'Good dog; there's a good boy; all right, my boy!' very warmly, as described for reassuring a dog on page 203— not because this book tells you to—but because you are genuinely trying to soothe him and communicate with him!

Your dog must not get any further away from you, because this will reinforce his fear. An outstretched hand of encouragement may help to calm him down, and encourage him to come toward you.

If you hold the lead firmly, keep calm and relaxed, and speak to him *very* warmly; he'll realize sooner or later both that there's nothing to be afraid of—and that there's no escape. He will either stop and look at you or come creeping forward, drawn by your relaxed and loving attitude, and by the warmth in your voice.

Even if he stops for only a moment—praise him immediately! Praise him warmly *and* gently so as not to scare him back in to his antics, and yet still to convey to him that he's *very* clever to stop prancing about.

(There's no need to say, of course, that you don't tug, pull, punish, command, shout or even move toward your dog at any stage of this exercise.)

Let him come *all* the way to you. If he stops just short of you, you can put out a hand to touch him to reassure him, and he may come for more petting when you withdraw it. But rather than move *to* him, move *away* from him and he'll probably want to follow you. Don't stand up yet, or you'll startle him.

No doubt, he'll return to his acrobatics. Continue to offer him reassurance when he starts bucking and squealing again, and rewarding him when he stops.

When he finds that he can trust you, he'll come to you more readily—especially if you keep relaxed and calm, speaking very warmly and lovingly to him.

If at any time your dog refuses to come to you, in spite of being relaxed and loving, gently hold his scruff on each side of his neck, and pull him on to your lap—and *praise* him! Move back, say 'Good dog!', and see if he comes on to your lap again for more praise! While you're rewarding him, edge back. When you find he's willing to stay with you as you move back slowly, he should like his praise enough to keep with you as you start gradually moving faster, until he's actually walking on the lead.

Do this once a day for a few minutes only.

When, at last, at the start of a session, instead of rushing to the other end of the lead, he comes straight to you for the praise he knows he'll get, you can start walking with him slowly, bending over him at first to give him confidence, patting him and praising each step warmly and extravagantly.

He should turn into a very willing worker, provided he gets very light correction (if any)— and abundant, warm and loving praise.

16. Chasing cats and livestock

As described in the section on biting, fighting and car chasing, the culprit must receive a punishment which exceeds the intensity of the excitement created by the situation of killing and chasing, otherwise the punishment will not be effective.

Provided your dog isn't a hardened culprit, you should be able to cure him.

First of all, give him a strict and carefully conducted training routine, so that he becomes accustomed to applying self-control.

(a) Cats

When your dog has had some training, tell him to sit and stay—and then tie him securely to a post. Be ready with a ruler or coat-hanger to hit him on his nose with. Place the cat in front of him and tell him sharply to 'Leave!'

The *very instant* he makes a move towards the cat, repeat the 'Leave!' command and clobber him. The poor cat won't like this exercise very much, but if you do it properly she'll benefit in the long run.

Restore trust and repeat again—if Puss can take it, and if you can find her!

If you're disturbed by the punishment you have to give your dog, you'll observe that in such a state of extreme excitement, caused by the instinct to give chase, he feels surprisingly little discomfort. And, as for his nose—nature built it to stand up to tougher treatment than that. Anyway, his nose suffers less than the cat would if she were caught! If your dog doesn't turn his head in pain or put it down, or rub his nose with his paw, or show some sort of reaction to the punishment, it wasn't hard enough. If he just ignores you and tries to give chase, you're being much too soft with him.

Every time you punish your dog adequately—and he feels very sorry for himself—pet him instantly; he must have *that* to look forward to, to help him resist the temptation to chase the cat.

When, after placing the cat in front of him, you notice that he glances at you instead of taking a dive at her, *reward him as if he's absolutely brilliant*—in fact throw your arms around him as if he's a hero!

During future exercises, you can then punish your dog for so much as even giving the cat a dark look. His eyes will either reveal whether he's completely lost the desire to chase, or betray his urge to do so. If you reward his every effort to restrain himself, and punish his every bad thought, he can become completely reformed. Do this for about two minutes once a day until he's cured.

(b) Chickens

Follow more or less the same procedure. The clucking and flapping of chickens, however, excite a dog far more than the running of a cat. Instead of throwing a chicken down in front of him, let him walk around in the chicken run on a lead which you hold in your left hand, while you hold the ruler in your right. Get that punishment in *fast* or he'll wrench himself free and make a meal of a hen in no time.

If he persists in only *looking* good, but not in *being* good (i.e. only chasing them when you're not around), try tying him to a very strong post for a whole day with water to drink, in a shady spot in the chicken-run—

secure him *very* firmly with a strong check chain. Use only the type of lead shown in chapter 9; or he's sure to break free and there'll be one gleeful dog and no hens. Even if he spends the whole day straining at the end of his lead, with a bit of luck, he won't want to look another bird in the eye again for the rest of his life.

Take him on a conducted tour around the chicken-run the next day. If he appears to take no interest in the hens (the expression in his eyes will betray whether or not he's trying to con you) you either give up or let him do another stretch! However, he probably won't show any interest in the chickens any more Reward him for ignoring them. Bend over him, hug him, pat him, praise him—anything, as long as he gets the message that *that's* what's expected of him!

(c) *Other livestock*

You'll be unlikely to cure a confirmed killer of large livestock. Like a fighting dog, the last thing he'll surrender before his life will be his urge to kill. He should either be sold to a city household (provided, that is, that he has enough space, and that he's not a biter or a fighter as well) or put down.

17. Roaming

No dog should be allowed to roam freely. In towns he could easily have, or cause, an accident and even in the country he could worry livestock. Confirmed roamers often seem very capable of handling traffic and looking after themselves. Locking up this type of dog won't please him, because the challenge of new smells, romps with his pals, seeking new bitches and scrounging titbits from favourite shopowners, make life at home very dull by comparison. He is happy and self-sufficient. Don't put yourself in a position where you have to punish him by locking him up. Always keep him under control so that he does not become a roamer.

A dog that roams is either a dog of superior intelligence that has potential and ability, and finds life at home does not provide him with the challenge and interest he needs or, he has a well-developed sense of smell, and finds those faraway scents irresistible. He can't stay at home and snooze when those scents waft over and tempt him to get up and go out and investigate!

And lastly, there's the chap that's out after sex.

(1) The first type of roamer can be encouraged to stay home if his family provide him with the interest he needs, and the potential he's capable of. If being part of the family indoors with them, outings with them, supervised walks, games and training fulfil him he'll stay at home.

(2) The second type of roamer is usually a hunting dog, often of pack origin, and may even find other dogs more interesting than you! Perhaps getting him a pal (of the opposite sex) will encourage him to stay at home. Also, let him become part of the family and provide him with games and interests as suggested above, to help keep him at home.

(3) Casanovas may also find a girl friend at home, games, training and so on incentive to roam less. Castration is discussed on page 165. If you are desperate, I suggest you resort to this. People who have tried it have been very thrilled with having a dog around the house again.

Lastly—punishing your dog for roaming when he comes home will make him think twice before he comes home after his next outing!

18. Refusal to eat

A healthy dog may refuse to eat: in the hopes that something better will be dished up; because he has an over-anxious owner; because this way he gets lots of attention; or he's genuinely upset, and is reacting for the same reason that a dog reverts to messing indoors; or because he's getting lousy food—or for all these reasons.

If your dog drinks milk, give him a bowl each day with a little complete dog meal in it. Gradually increase the amount of solids you put into his milk until he's eating properly.

If he won't drink milk, the best advice is—relax. Find him a reasonably tasty food—some tinned dog meat, or mince mixed with meal, for example. Force-feed him with a few mouthfuls each day, then put the dish down and leave it down for half an hour.

Go out of the room and ignore him. Don't draw any attention to the food on the floor, or hang around to see if he's going to eat it.

The food you're forcing into his stomach will stimulate his appetite again, and give him strength. A dog that refuses to eat for ages can lose his appetite altogether and become weak and ill.

To force-feed your dog, place his food-bowl near by hold a ball of food in your right hand and straddle him. With his bottom jaw in your left hand, hold his head up. Lift his top jaw and put the food far back in his throat with your right hand. If necessary, grip him firmly with your knees, and hold his head up until he swallows. To make him swallow, stroke his throat, or pour a spoonful of milk down his throat. If you talk to him soothingly and keep relaxed, he'll be less likely to struggle. Give him three or four mouthfuls twice day, increasing the quantity until he eats on his own.

But as long as you watch over your dog and coax him he won't eat; so forget about it for the rest of the day.

You can, for extra nourishment, give your dog some yeast tablets, or a bowl of glucose water, or Complan and milk, or let him lick Marmite off your finger.

If your dog is small, it may be that he has a very small appetite and you have nothing to worry about anyway.

19. Stealing food and begging

A course of training never did a canine thief any harm because, more than likely, he's somewhat unmanageable as well.

After several training sessions, tell your dog to sit and stay. Then put some tempting food on a table about 3 metres away from him. Tell him to 'Leave!' and walk out of the room for one second. Come back *instantly* and reward him for not touching it—even though he hasn't had a chance! If he tries, reprimand him sharply or punish him, depending on his temperament—as long as the correction you give him is worth avoiding.

Each time you return and find he hasn't touched the food, act as if he's a genius. Say '*That's* a clever dog!', hug him, pat him and so on.

Do this once a day, going out of sight three or four times on each session, increasing the length of time, starting at about one second, and *very* gradually working up to about fifteen seconds over the weeks.

Never leave your dog too near to the food, and it must never become too difficult for him, or he'll never be able to learn. Never give him the food he resisted stealing, or he'll get impatient during the exercise—and help himself.

Do not, for example, expect your dog to resist stealing the cat's steakmince left on the floor, when he gets a meatless diet. You're unlikely to be able to feed him the same diet as your cat, so keep the cat's food out of temptation's way, or he'll become sly. *Too* much temptation might be too much for *anyone*!

To break the habit of begging, however, lock your dog out of the room while you're eating—and, of course, don't give him any more titbits from the table.

20. Raiding dust-bins, rolling in dirt, and eating dirt

If your dog is properly fed, and still raids dust-bins, he should be cured of this habit—it's easier to cure him than it is to clean up after him! Tying the lid on the bin won't be kept up after it's been tied and untied several times a day, so if your dog only does it at night, feed him in the evening and let him sleep inside. If he does it first thing in the morning when he's let out, watch him and, while he's busy, throw a stone to clank on the bin, and send him scurrying away in fright. A few times should change his ways.

But some dogs only raid their neighbours' bins—and creeping around the neighbourhood at 5.00 a.m., stone in hand, isn't a pastime most people would relish. Apologize nicely to your neighbour, hand him a stone, and give him full permission to hit dog or bin if he catches the culprit in the act. He'll be only too pleased to oblige. Your dog will begin to leave the bin alone only if he develops very unpleasant associations with it. Give him a nice juicy bone when he comes home, tail between his legs, bruised and sorry for himself.

If your dog tears open black plastic bags used in some areas, keep him in for those few minutes before they're collected. It's rather like being tempted with Kitty's meat as described above—a little too difficult for a dog to resist.

Rolling in dirt is another story. Your dog is a dog and it's a reflex that sends him rolling on his back when he smells something that you and he have directly opposite opinions on. Bath him—with rubber gloves on—in Dettol. If you live on a farm, you'll do it often. But he won't understand if you try to teach him not to.

Fortunately, not all dogs develop this habit.

Eating filth is just as bad, but, like I said—a dog is a dog.

21. Barking at the gate and fence

If your dog spends much of his time doing this, he's bored and needs exercise. Both are dealt with at length in previous sections of this chapter.

Your dog must also learn to come to you when you want to call him away from his activity. (See chapter 10.) As his excitement is pretty extreme when you command him, he'll need a severe punishment. Punish him with a slipper or a clod, as suggested and, of course, restore trust. A confirmed runner-up-and-down-of-fences has built up strong muscles and has plenty of energy, and when you want to punish him or catch him, you'll find he's also built up a great sense of enjoyment from his pastime, and will dodge all attempts at either.

Never try to chase or catch your dog; he has a distinct advantage over you, and knows it! Command and correct him only when you're near enough to be heard easily an can get a good aim. Make his corrections worth avoiding, and his rewards very exciting.

A training programme—during which you develop a good relationship with your dog, as well as making him submissive—will give you a much better chance of persuading him to drop this vice. But you must give him companionship as well as another outlet for his excess energy—supervised exercise, ball games, and so on.

22. Yapping

A dog that stands and yaps for no apparent reason, usually does it out of habit, or boredom, or both. If his yapping is hysterical, perhaps he can't see clearly, and is disturbed and frightened by what he imagines he sees. If your dog has long hair growing over his eyes, keep the hair clipped so that he can see properly. And a dog that has extra-sensitive hearing will bark at all the faraway sounds, and should sleep indoors.

If your dog won't stop barking when you call him, arm yourself with a bowl of water or a large clod. Without letting him spot you, get near to him and command him: 'Jason, quiet!' Don't shout, but command him crisply, as demonstrated. If your dog holds his peace—reward him profusely and call him inside. But if your command didn't make him stop barking, throw your weapon—and restore trust. If you've startled him, you'll have to crouch down when you restore trust. (If you use water, it'll be more effective if you throw it in his face.) For those who have slow timing, simply command and throw together.

After your dog has experienced this a couple of times, your command alone should be sufficient to make him desist. But you must *always* reward him immediately, preferably crouching down to bring him to you—make it really worth his while to obey.

The punishment *must* be unpleasant, or he'll simply remove himself to where he can resume his barking out of range.

A dog that barks at night can be brought inside where the outdoor noises and smells don't stimulate him into wakefulness; after all, it's not fair to the neighbours. A noisy dog indoors is dealt with in chapter 2, assuming, of course, that he's not warning his family of an intruder! I wonder how many dogs are told to 'Shut up!' while the burglar gets on with his business!

. . . over-demanding . . .

23. Over-possessive and over-demanding dogs

Over-possessiveness is an expression of insecurity in a dog. He shadows his owner, making constant demands on his or her attention. He needs both authoritative, firm, decisive handling and intense, warm, loving handling.

Training, properly carried out, should help this type of dog. If you can meet his *need* for love and attention completely, and punish his *greed* for too much, you'll go a long way towards making him more secure.

If you don't meet his need, he'll fight through all your attempts to punish him. But you *must* punish his greed, or he'll never become secure and nor will you be able to endure his excessive demands. It's *knowing* where he stands that helps him to feel secure—he gets all the love he needs and knows what's expected of him.

When a dog greets his owner, or comes for a pat, a few moments' undivided attention, and a loving greeting (it's the *quality*, not the *quantity* that he will appreciate) followed by 'Lie down!' is all he wants. And until he gets it he'll be a pest, despite all corrections and reprimands.

When a dog's demands are *too* excessive he is probably unsuited to his owner (and vice versa)—this is discussed in the section on choosing a dog to suit your temperament.

24. Fear of riding in a car

A dog may be afraid to get into a car after he's had some unpleasant experience, because he expects a visit to the vet or kennels—or because he's never been in one. To cure a dog of this, follow the programme described in chapter 3, for curing a dog of car-sickness. To get the dog in, a small dog can easily be picked up before he even suspects there's a car ride in the offing, then taken to the car and put in. Don't allow him to escape before all the doors are shut, or his fear will be reinforced. Give him a tasty morsel, and let him jump out. Do this once a day until he begins to jump in eagerly for his titbit. Then, take him for a short ride, but a second person should be present to soothe him and keep him on the back seat in case he jumps around and causes an accident.

Only drive a very short way, and then give him a game or run on his return. Repeat this once a day, until he looks forward to the ride, as suggested on page 99.

However, it's much more difficult with a large dog.

To teach a large dog to get used to a car, put the tasty morsel just at the entrance of an open car door, and leave him to take it of his own accord. If you try to coax him, or stand near by, he'll be suspicious and won't go near. You may even have to put the titbit near the car on the ground and slowly, over the days, or weeks, put it closer each time, until it's *in* the car.

When your dog has come to realize that you're not going to try to catch him, he'll be less suspicious. When he finally jumps into the car for the food, *do not* close the door on him. *Let him jump straight out again.* Only close the door and drive away when he's quite happy to jump in and out. This can only be achieved if you're very patient and remain quite relaxed about the whole thing.

Then follow the routine of short rides with something to look forward to at the other end of each journey. It may all take some weeks or even months to achieve.

Should you need to take your dog somewhere in the car before he's got used to it, put him on a lead, then, with the help of a couple of strong hands, lift him in. Someone should be ready to receive him, and to hold him on the back seat during the ride. Shut the car door as soon as he's in, leaving most of the lead outside, secured to the outer door handle.

If your dog is very afraid, be firm with him and soothe him. If necessary, ask your vet for a tranquillizer to give to him before his car ride.

25. Canine Casanovas

A dog that's perpetually mounting other dogs and objects is not only a misery to himself but an embarrassment to his owners. The dog may have an infection, such as an infected prostate gland or be oversexed, all of

which your vet can diagnose. Arranging a love affair
will probably make him worse—because then he'll know
what it's all about.

If your dog is oversexed your vet can give him hormone
injections to relieve his condition. Castration is discussed
on page 165. If your dog doesn't respond to injections of
hormones, I would suggest you have him castrated. It
will be a relief to both you and your dog.

It's quite natural, however, for pups—both male and
female—to mount one another in play. If they cause
embarrassment, just reprimand them. If it becomes
excessive, however, it should be dealt with by injections
or castration.

26. Ball hysteria

If your dog develops an hysterial attitude towards
throwing games, stop throwing balls for him altogether.

He may even refuse to go for a walk unless he has
a ball thrown for him. Just ignore him until he gives up
asking, and enjoys his outing. If he keeps bringing balls
or ball substitutes to you, he's obviously a dog that needs
plenty of exercise, and needs more opportunity to release
his pent-up energy.

Many dogs thoroughly enjoy throwing games, and
they cause no problems. But occasionally a dog's obses-
sion with chasing borders on insanity and he can think
of nothing else—then it's best to put him out of his
frustrated misery, and get a dog that will bring more
pleasure.

27. Insanity

This isn't easily defined or recognized in a dog.
Repeated fits; repeated hysterical tail chasing (which is
not in play or as a result of any irritation); sudden outbursts of barking at nothing, accompanied by a wild

staring gaze (probably the equivalent of hallucinations in people); constant licking at the air (an uncontrollable nervous reaction); unreasonable fear; a glazed, distant look in the eyes, usually seen in a dog that doesn't respond readily to caresses; are all symptoms of a disturbed mind, which, unfortunately, is incurable.

These reactions may be observed in a dog that has undergone an extremely distressing experience and become permanently unhinged. A terrifying journey, long hours spent alone, ill-treatment, may, for instance, be the cause. A dog may also have inherited his insanity from his parents, or he may have a physical condition, such as a tumour.

Needless to say, there's only one course of action. Put the dog out of his misery and get a companion that will bring you pleasure, and not anxiety.

Should you be considering replacing your dog with one of the same breed, avoid another pup from the same kennel, or with ancestors in common—should the condition be hereditary.

28. Incurable disobedience

When a dog is deliberately disobedient, despite all training, and he has been trained and corrected for his misdemeanours as suggested, I don't think it's worth keeping him, and turning your whole life upside down with the domestic ructions such a dog causes.

There is the occasional dog that will resist all correction. It may just be that he has very high spirits and his owners are no match for him, or he may be a selfish, cunning and calculating dog. The layman's 'cure-all' for this type of dog is: send him to a farm. But not only is the farmer also wanting a dog he can handle but his livestock will probably be endangered,

Rather than try to tolerate the inconvenience such a dog brings—or turn him loose on some unsuspecting family by giving him away—ask the vet to put him out of your misery.

CHAPTER 18

GIVING AWAY
OR SELLING A DOG

Whether you are selling your bitch's pups, are having to part with your pet, or are finding a home for a stray, you should find a few tips in this chapter to help you select a suitable home.

When prospective buyers make enquiries, consider them carefully. You have the right to know what fate is awaiting the dog you've raised, loved and cared for. If your dog is large, can they afford to feed him, and is their property spacious enough for him? Is it perhaps unfenced and on a busy road where he probably won't last very long? Will he be at the mercy of a crowd of undisciplined children? Do they work all day, so that he'll be lonely, and if he's a pup, go without his midday meal? Will he be allowed indoors? If the pup is taken indoors into the heart of his new home, he'll be much happier than if he's either left to roam or become lonely and bored in a backyard on his own or, have they perhaps too many dogs already?

What happened to their last dog? If, for instance, he was put to sleep at a ripe old age, your dog will stand a much better chance with them than if he goes to a family that has dogs that are continually being run over.

And, lastly, the section on choosing a dog to suit your temperament will guide you on tactfully deciding not to give a Pyrenean Mountain dog, which unexpectedly outgrew a suburban home, to Gran and Gramps

in a city flat! If you are placing a litter, this section will be particularly helpful in finding owners that will be temperamentally compatible with your pups.

Once you've chosen the new owners for your dog, tell them what he's been used to eating; if he's an adult dog tell them what games he likes to play, and so on. And suggest they buy a copy of this book.

Dogs of any age, short of old age, can settle down surprisingly well in a new home. But those that shrink into themselves and cower away in a corner, refusing to eat when parted from their owner, should rather be put down than given away. These reactions may mean nothing for a day or two, but if the dog shows no signs of accepting a new owner after four or five days, it's obvious that he'll never adjust to a new home. Fortunately, dogs that react in this manner are rare.

The original owners of a fully-grown dog should never visit him, as this will confuse him and make him unsettled.

A lot of dogs are given away free, but somehow human nature is such that it values more what it has paid for.

It's not necessary to say, I'm sure, that giving away a dog because he fights, bites, chases cars, or knocks everyone over, is only solving the problem for you, but the dog takes these problems to his next home, and the poor owners who inherit him have only difficulties and disappointment in store for them.

Lastly, you may like to suggest that if after a few days the dog is not found to be suitable you'll take him back, rather than let his new owners try to make the best of a bad situation, or take him to an animal sanctuary, where he may be confined in kennels for a long time before he's finally placed—or even put down. It'll be more trouble for you to find a more suitable home for him, but he still has his whole life ahead of him.

INDEX

316